Boston Deep Sea Fisheries

The Story of One of Britain's Major Fishing Companies

by

Mark Stopper and Ray Maltby

Hutton Press
1995

Published by

The Hutton Press Ltd.,
130 Canada Drive, Cherry Burton,
Beverley HU17 7SB

Printed by
Image Colourprint Ltd.,
Grange Park Lane,
Willerby, Hull HU10 6EB

ISBN 1 872167 68 3

Contents

Acknowledgements

During the preparation of this book we have had cause to contact many people throughout the British Isles. The response has been tremendous and most helpful. The number involved is many more than we can include here, but to all those people we extend our grateful and sincere thanks because without their help this work would not have been possible.

We have included many photographs and again we are overwhelmed by the helpful response of copyright owners who have allowed their pictures to be used. To them our grateful thanks. For some of the older photographs and a few later ones used, we were not able to trace origins; therefore we have been forced to list them as the Mark Stopper collection.

There are a few people to whom we would like to offer our special thanks as, without their help, this work would never have been possible. Peter Catchpole, Managing Director of Boston Putford Offshore Safety Ltd. Arthur Credland, Keeper of Maritime History Town Docks Museum, Hull. Alec Gill, himself a published author. The Grimsby Evening Telegraph. The late Jack Mitchley of the Port of Lowestoft Research Society. Michael Thompson, another published author, and we would not wish to forget our friend, Steve Pulfrey who has been most helpful throughout.

Finally there are two distinguished gentlemen who knew everything from the inside of Boston Deep Sea Fisheries. They are, of course, the late Sir Basil Parkes, O.B.E. and his son Neil, both of whom were extremely helpful. To them our most grateful thanks, with a special thank you to Neil who has generously agreed to write the foreword to our work.

March 1995.

Foreword
by
Neil Parkes

Mark Stopper and Ray Maltby's book on the history of Boston Deep Sea Fisheries is a well researched and fascinating record of the Company from its early days in Boston, through much of this century until the virtual collapse of the Corporate Sector of the British Fishing Industry in the early 1980s, as a result of international fishing limit extensions and the Common Fisheries Policy restrictions. The book records in great detail the multitude of vessels that comprised the Boston Fleet and their various Ports of operation, as well as highlighting some of the principal characters who contributed to the Company's success, both ashore and afloat.

Sadly not enough history of the Fishing Industry in general has been properly recorded and now with the passage of time many of the great leaders of the Industry have passed on, taking their knowledge with them, and it is therefore a great credit to Mark Stopper and Ray Maltby that they should have endeavoured to record the history of one Company and its fleet of vessels. The Boston Company was a major player in the Industry from the early years of this century throughout the whole period. My Grandfather, Sir Fred Parkes, was extremely cautious in his approach which ensured a successful growth of the Company and was ably backed by my father, Sir Basil Parkes, who was more pioneering than his father and always endeavoured to keep the Company in the forefront of technical developments in the Industry. Innovation can be expensive as not every development is necessarily successful in the early stages and Mark Stopper and Ray Maltby's book records many of the technical innovations which took place, some of which were entirely successful and others less so. It represents an admirable record of one Company which played a major part in a once great Industry.

The
BOSTON DEEP SEA FISHING AND ICE Co.,
LIMITED

❦ BALANCE SHEET, ❧

31st MARCH, 1887.

Liabilities.	£	s	d	Assets.	£	s	d
To Capital Account :—				By Construction Account :—Steam and			
3313 Shares of £10 each 33130 0 0				Sailing Trawlers, Buildings,			
Less Calls in arrear ... 69 0 0				Machinery, Tools, Plant, Office			
				Furniture, &c.	49466	17	11
	33361	0	0	,, Sundry Debtors on open accounts ...	1062	8	2½
,, Loans on Debentures...	17000	0	0	,, Cash in hand	90	11	8
,, Interest on ditto, accrued due to date	389	6	2	,, Stock on hand viz :—			
,, Sundry Creditors on open accounts ...	1924	3	3½	Fitters, Tinners, and			
,, Garfit, Claypon & Co.,				Smiths Departments 427 15 2			
as per pass books 5073 10 2				Sailmakers do. 170 19 9			
Add cheques not presented 40 2 1				Mast and Block			
	5113	12	3	Makers do. 221 19 4			
				Twine Spinners do. 78 11 8			
				Stores do. 1072 19 2			
				Ice do. 424 1 0			
				Stage, Kits, &c. 73 11 10			
					2469	17	11
				,, Insurance Account :—Amount paid			
				in advance	1351	0	5
				,, Formation expenses	647	19	10
				,, Suspense Account :—Ansell's Trial...	64	18	8
				,, Balance as per Profit & Loss Account	2634	7	1
	£57,788	**1**	**8¼**		**£57,788**	**1**	**8¼**

PROFIT AND LOSS ACCOUNT.

	£	s	d		£	s	d
To Balance, 31st March, 1886	1246	10	6	By Smacks' Earnings	2710	6	6
,, Loss per Smack "Humber" ...	600	0	0	,, Steamers' do.	18472	15	0½
,, Smacks' Expenses	3411	14	11	,, Commission	1084	17	10
,, Steamers' do.	17256	15	2	Gain on Departments, viz :—			
,, Insurance	1891	8	6	Fitters, Tinners, and			
,, Interest :—Bank, &c. ... 347 17 7				Smiths 389 15 2			
Debenture ... 850 15 8				Sailmaking ... 9 13 9			
	1198	13	3	Mast and Block 412 3 11			
,, Salaries...	776	11	0	Twine Spinning ... 498 0 8½			
,, General Expenses	313	4	0	Stores 235 8 6			
,, Rates, Taxes, Rents, &c. ...	79	15	6	Ice 588 15 3½			
,, Law Charges	55	1	0		2134	6	4
,, Collision Account	23	4	0	,, Salvage Account	80	17	2
,, Stage do.	3	12	6	,, Balance	2634	7	1
,, Bad Debts	210	19	7½				
	£27,067	**9**	**11¼**		**£27,067**	**9**	**11¼**

I hereby certify that the above is a correct Statement of the Company's Accounts as shewn by their Books on the 31st day of March 1887,

ROBT. HODGSON,
16, Parliament Street, Hull,
AUDITOR.

16th May 1887.

Boston Deep Sea Fishing & Ice Co., Balance sheet for 31st. March 1887. Photo courtesy Grimsby Library.

Chapter One

Boston – The Formative Years

The first Boston company was initiated at a meeting held at Boston Guild Hall on 7th. August 1885. The Boston Deep Sea Fishing & Ice Co. was formed with a capital of £60,000, available as 6,000 shares of 10 each. 4,000 shares were to be issued immediately with the other 2,000 being held in reserve for future use. The initial subscribers were Thomas Cheyney Garfit (200 shares), Thomas Slater (10 shares), William John Pilcher (25 shares), Thomas Kitwood (25 shares), A.H. Read (5 shares), W.M. Cooper (10 shares) and C. Yeatman (10 shares). The first board of Directors included four of the above and was composed as follows:-

Chairman - Thomas Cheyney Garfit Esq. of Messrs. Garfit, Claypon & Co. of Boston.
Directors - Richard Millington Esq., Mayor of Boston.
  Walter T. Small Esq. of Bargate Lodge, Boston.
  William John Pilcher Esq. Surgeon of Boston.
  Thomas Kitwood Esq. Wine & Spirit Merchant, Boston.
  John M. Simpson Esq. of Boston.
  Thomas Slater Esq., Merchant & Ship Chandler, Boston.
  Alfred Wheatley Ansell Esq. Wholesale Fish & Ice
  Merchant, Hull.

The company's bankers were Messrs. Garfit Claypon & Co. of Boston or their agents, Lloyds. Barnetts & Bosanquets of Lombard Street, London. Messrs. Millington Simpson of Boston were appointed solicitors whilst Messrs. Jacks, Hodgson & Jacks of Change Alley, Cornhill, London were to act as brokers. The offices were at 29, Wide Bargate, Boston. The formation of the new company was advertised in numerous daily newspapers and Sacks & Co. were engaged by the company for a fee of £105 on condition that they issue a minimum of 1,000 shares.

Alfred Wheatley Ansell was appointed the first Managing Director as part of a deal in which he would sell the company seven fishing smacks, *Angela*, *Atlanta*, *Caledonia*, *Crusader*, *Hibernia* and *Scotia*, for £9,000 on condition that he took the 100 fully paid shares, and that that £2,000 of the cost was left as a first mortgage on the vessels. His salary was to be £1 per smack per week until the 1st. January 1886 when it would become £800 per annum. Ansell also undertook to move to the Boston area for which he was to receive £300 compensation. He was also to receive 5% commission on sales of fish and ice other than the fish sent to inland markets on commission.

The new company was not content with acquiring second-hand sailing smacks and at a board meeting, held on the 27th. August, only 20 days after its formation, ordered two new steam trawlers from Earles of Hull. They were launched in November 1885 with the builders requiring payment in full on delivery. Although the company was giving the impression of having limitless funds, it wasn't long before the directors found it necessary to dip into their own pockets. Cheyney Garfit loaned the company £8,000 with the other directors contributing smaller amounts and this was not the last time their generosity would be called upon. Most of the early Boston vessels were only insured for two thirds of their cost.

There being no facilities for handling large cargoes of fish at Boston, the company's first vessels were initially based at Hull. Negotiations between the company and Boston Corporation eventually procured an agreement with the docks works committee that the latter would build a fish quay and stores. Constructed on the south side of the dock basin the fish quay was to be 200ft. long and 90ft. wide. Permission was also granted for the construction of a telegraph office which was to have a direct line to the main Post Office. The Boston Company undertook to build engineering workshops at a cost £558 and equip them with machinery to the value of £2,000. This was financed by various directors and shareholders lending £500 on mortgages.

By March 1886, the Grimsby news was predicting the imminent movement of vessels from Hull to Boston. An April 1886 issue of the *Illustrated London News* carried a graphic of the arrival of the company's first trawlers at Boston, whilst *Ingram's* magazine reported, "Their arrival had been looked forward to with no little expectation". Bright sunlight greeted the four vessels, *Witham, Holland, Kesteven* and *Lindsey,* as they steamed up the River Witham on the afternoon tide, whilst at the newly completed fish quay, thousands of people were assembled to welcome the newcomers. Only one of the vessels was returning from a fishing trip, the other three having sailed down from Hull with their crews, their families and their furniture. The first catch of fish was landed and sold the next morning.

At a board meeting later the same month, it was agreed that it was essential to to provide a daily supply of fish if Boston was to thrive as a fishing port. If this was to happen it was essential to replace the sailing smacks with more steam trawlers. Already the sailing smack was beginning to fade from the scene, partly because the new steam trawlers were not restricted by the

The Boston company's Fish Pontoon with offices and workshops on the first floor. Photo courtesy Dave Simpson Studio.

One of the Company's early steam trawlers, the Skirbeck BN 81, lying alongside the old wooden jetty which remains today. Photo courtesy Dave Simpson Studio.

fickleness of the weather as were the sailing ships and partly because of the capacity of the new vessels, together with the ability to harness the steam to the winches to speed shooting and hauling the trawl net. Two new vessels were sanctioned and these were duly ordered from W. Holmes of Hull in June at a cost of £3,420 each. At a later meeting it was necessary to call for a further £1 per share from the shareholders.

The August 27th. 1886 issue of the *Grimsby Mercury*, reported thus:- "The Boston Deep Sea Fishing & Ice Company was floated a short time ago with as fair a prospect before as any trading venture could have. The capital was readily subscribed and the port was all that could be desired for fishing vessels. Every body was well disposed towards the new company, and the market for the harvest of the sea was practically unlimited. It is feared, however, that the most is not being made of the opportunity which the company enjoys and rumours, which we hope may prove to be fabrication, are being circulated about the conditions of the trawlers that the company purchased, in a hurry, and at a great cost last year. We allude to the matter here, because it is one of great public interest to Bostonians individually, and because the company, if successfully worked, must of necessity confer considerable benefit on the town as a whole. It is quite impossible that the company can be successful, however, unless it is worked with more method than has been shewn hitherto. Wholesale fish salesmen complain that there is no regular supply of fish they have come to the town to purchase, and say that, unless there is a speedy alteration, they will be compelled to leave Boston for some other market, where they can depend upon being able to execute their customers orders, with something like regularity. We have mentioned that rumours are afloat as to the conditions of the company's trawlers, but we refrain from giving additional currency to them. It is, we hope, impossible that they are true, for the truth would mean that the company has been grossly and shamelessly imposed upon by the vendor of the trawlers and also that its directors are incompetent. In the interests of the town and for the sake of the Company's shareholders we trust that these rumours are without foundation".

On the face of it, a friendly warning to the people of Boston, but one cannot help but reflect that, in modern terminology, Grimsby was "putting the boot in while the man was down". After all, if Boston was to thrive as a fishing port, it would probably be at the expense of other ports, and possibly Grimsby felt that it was most vulnerable. Especially as one of the directors, the vendor of the fishing vessels alluded to in the article, came from Hull as even then there was little love lost between the Humber ports.

However, there is no smoke without fire and it soon became apparent that all was not well with the company. Alfred Ansell was dismissed as Managing Director for what appears to be gross misuse of his position. In the court case that inevitably followed, the company sued Ansell and another man, Hadfield, over unsatisfactory accounts and improper payments, whilst Ansell claimed damages for unfair dismissal. Among the charges were ones of receiving bonuses from the Hull Ice Co. and the Hull Steam Fishing Co. and commission from Messrs. Earles for placing the order for two steam trawlers with them. There was also a question mark over the condition of some of the fishing smacks and the price paid for them. It was in the surveying of the vessels that Hadfield was involved. Ansell strongly denied any underhand practices and claimed £1,000 damages but settled for £781 out of court. It would appear from the Chairman's comments at the annual shareholders meeting in May 1888 that although the company had paid the damages and also their own legal costs they had still to pay the defendant, Ansell's costs. Ansell attended the meeting and attempted to ask some searching questions about mortgages. The board were able to answer these satisfactorily. The manager appointed in Ansell's place, Captain John Mountain, received a salary of £150 per annum.

In April 1887 it was reported that Boston Trawler crews were trading some of their catch at sea in exchange for gin and whisky which they then proceeded to smuggle into the port. The company issued a warning to all their crews that a repetition of those offences would lead to instant dismissal. Cheyney Garfit again came to the aid of the ailing company with a £3,000 loan, secured by a mortgage on company properties. This loan was repaid during the same year.

It was at the third annual general meeting of the company, held in the Town Hall at Boston at the end of May 1888, when Cheyney Garfit reported on the costs of the Ansell case, that the issued share capital was given as £33,430, turnover of £49,466 with a declared trading profit of £2,600. The steam trawler fleet was by then ten strong, with eight of the old sailing trawlers used only in the summer months. Other advantageous assets were the engineering and fitting shops and block making, together with the company's advent into sailmaking and twine and rope spinning shops. Ice was shipped from Norway in 500 ton cargoes at 13 shillings per ton and stored in the company's own ice storage facility. Best hard steam coal was obtained through the

TRAWLERS AT THE DOCK

Local people greet the return to port of two of Boston's trawlers as they wait in the lock pit for a berth. The young lad on the quayside looks on with keen interest, probably contemplating a future at sea. Photo courtesy Dave Simpson Studio.

Hull coal merchants, Bielby's, at 8 shillings and 8 pence per ton. It had already been decided in February 1888 to dispose of the sailing smacks and the prudence of this was shown by the fact that the steam trawlers regularly returned a profit while the sailing vessels were consistently showing a loss. Negotiations commenced in August, the company obviously deciding to have one final summer out of them, then seven, *Angela, Atlanta, Caledonia, Crusader, Hibernia, Rover* and *Scotia* were sold for £1,275 to the Grimsby Ice Co. They transferred to Grimsby registry in the autumn of 1888. Five were later to see service out of Great Yarmouth, the other two being lost. It is also worthy of note that only the *Humber* is missing from the seven smacks purchased from Ansell for £9,000 only three years earlier. This vessel had been wrecked on the notorious Binks, just off Spurn Point, on the 7th. March 1886.

The huge loss the company appears to have made on the sale of those vessels was not necessarily because of their rundown condition, more likely it was a reflection of the fact that they were fast becoming obsolete, as the high-tech (to borrow a modern aphorism) steam trawlers entered service in ever-increasing numbers. Indeed, 1889 saw Boston's increasing their own fleet with orders being placed with Finch & Co. for two vessels at £4,100 each and later the same year a further two from Renoldson's of North Shields at £4,150 each. The following year saw orders for yet another pair, this time from Earle's of Hull costing £4,950 each.

The fortunes of the company were at last beginning to look up. After showing a trading loss in the first two years full trading and a small profit in 1888, by 1891 the company was able to declare a profit of £10,506 of which £6,262 was placed on credit to meet future depreciation. Return on capital for the company's shareholders had also taken some considerable time before coming to fruition with no dividends being paid until 1889 when 3% was granted, followed by 5% in 1890 and 10% in 1891. This figure was maintained in 1892 whilst the following two years showed a decrease with 7.5% and 8.5% being paid respectively. Much of the credit for this must be placed at the door of the company's able manager Capt. Mountain.

The company continued to prosper and during 1897 amalgamated with the Steam Trawling Co., a venture which increased the fleet to 24. Two further vessels were added during 1898. In the chairman's report given to the shareholders for the year ending 31st. 1899, held in the Guildhall, Boston in May of that year, Cheyney Garfit reported a profit of £12,520 after provision of £6,705 for depreciation. £6,000 was transferred to the reserve fund and a tax free dividend of 10% was paid to shareholders, leaving a balance of £1,061 to be carried forward. The chairman also praised the efforts of the general manager, Mr. J. Bloomfield, who had succeeded Capt. Mountain in 1897, and whose ability and business acumen had, in no small way, contributed to the current success of the company. Commenting on the transfer to reserve, Cheyney Garfit emphasised the fact that Boston fish prices were still lower than those at Grimsby, and although the company was still profitable, caution should be exercised against the hard times which could always be just around the corner. We, with the gift of hindsight, can realise how prophetic those words actually were when we consider the moribund condition of the company only 20 years later when its saviour appeared on the scene. In the same report, the chairman commented on differences of opinion between the company and the dock committee and Harbour Commissioners. He also criticised the Great Northern Railway Company for investing heavily in the docks at Grimsby where, "they only had a foothold on sufferance" instead of at Boston where they could have had a monopoly.

In 1900 the dominant position of the company was challenged with the advent of a new company with the creation of the Boston Steam Fishing Co. Although it has proved impossible to trace a report for the first year's trading of the new company, the report for the year ending 31st. 1902, the new company's 2nd. and the original Boston company's 18th., make interesting reading. The annual report of the Boston Deep Sea Fishing & Ice Co. once again showed a profit of £6,272, of which £5,469 was required to pay the 10% dividend, while the new company declared a profit of only £18. The Chairman of the new company, in his report, stated that, if the company was to survive, then either its vessels should be transferred to another port or, the company should amalgamate with the Boston Deep Sea Fishing & Ice Co. Hardly a glowing proposition for a new company, but by the middle of the decade, the company had passed into the control of its older neighbour.

The local newspaper, commenting on the success of the company at the turn of the century reported that it had "given a great fillip to the trade of the port, and it was said that Boston fish were appreciated far and wide" The paper also complimented the ability of its manager, James Bloomfield, whose endeavours had made it one of the most flourishing concerns in the county. In the same issue, the people of Boston were unfortunately reminded of the fragility of the hazardous life at sea with a report on the loss of the *Grampus*. Little over a year later, the same newspaper reported the loss of two crew members from different vessels. William Pull, a deckhand aboard *Flavian* had been struck on the chest by the anchor as it was being drawn over the side of the vessel; that incident occurred off the Faroe Islands. The second occurrence was much closer to home when Edward Chald, a steward aboard the *Brothertoft,* had fallen overboard and drowned off Spurn Point. Curiously, both men had recently moved to Boston from Grimsby in search of work and were making their first trips to sea on Boston ships.

Bloomfield was succeeded in 1902 by Frederick Donnison and although the company continued to trade successfully for a number of years, no dividends were paid after 1907 until 1917. By that time the company's saviour, (to whom I previously referred), because a saviour was certainly required, was a well known and respected Boston businessman, Mr. Fred Parkes.

Even before the outbreak of the First World War, the company had been in serious financial difficulties. The long serving solicitor, John Millington Simpson, at the annual general meeting in June 1923, recalled that several years previously he had informed the shareholders, the board's policy would be, never again to allow the company to succumb into the precarious position it found itself before the war when its assets were virtually at a dangerous level.

When it became obvious to them that their chances of successful trading were fading, John Millington thought the best advice to offer would be for the company to dissolve and return to the shareholders their share in the capital. Although things had improved for a short period after the first war, they were again on the decline.

John Millington Simpson had been connected with the company for thirty-eight years, during which time his object and that of his fellow directors had been to run the company giving priority to the benefit of the Borough rather than themselves. If a little profit was made for them, it was appreciated but their main objects remained to boost the trade for the town.

Born to a modestly poor family in the Sleaford area, Fred Parkes was one of six children whose early life included at least one night in the work-house. The family eventually settled in Boston where at a very young age he sold newspapers on the streets. Thus the young Fred, from below the bottom rung on the ladder, began to work his way to success. As a young man, by careful saving and extraordinary business acumen he bought out his employer's fish merchanting business when the owner died.

From there, he expanded into farming and trawler ownership. During the First World War he concentrated mainly on farming until, on cessation of hostilities, his interest developing in fishing, he saw the fish merchanting business resurrected. He also bought several new Admiralty ordered trawlers while they were still under construction.

Fred was elected to the board of the Boston Deep Sea Fishing & Ice Co. on the 8th. May 1919 by which time he already had several other interests. The trawlers he currently owned were fishing the North Sea very successfully and for quite a while Boston's had been losing some of their best men to him, but they were now handed over to the company at a modest profit. It was not long before Fred, using his gift of foresight tried desperately to persuade his co-directors to sell their old ships before they depreciated to only scrap value, then acquire a number of new vessels. At that time, two new ships could have been obtained for the price of three old ones. Any vessels acquired in that manner could, by taking advantage of the existing slipways in Boston plus their own engineering works, be modified to suit their requirements. However, Fred could not convince the other directors, their feeling being not only would the idea reduce the size of their fleet, it would also cost the jobs of some employees. The company was the largest employer in the town and the other directors were of the opinion they should continue to pursue that policy.

There now remained for Mr. Parkes only two alternatives, either he must leave the company or take control. He decided on the latter. His first manoeuvre was, with the backing of the bank, to buy up shares whenever he could. Using this ploy, before any of his co-directors realised, he soon had a 51% holding in the company which now gave him effective control and after several board meetings, on the 24th June 1924, he put himself in the chair. Most of the old directors left, leaving only Fred, and an old friend, Len Brocklesby, a shareholder, and Fred Anderson who had worked for Mr. Parkes since school-days.

Despite the fact that in 1919, it had only one trawler fishing, the company made the highest profit in its history. Expenses for that year were, for the steamers, £19,955 but their earnings totalled £56,344. Sadly those good fortunes were not consistent because the following year, although earnings rocketed by 140% to £132,353, expenses accelerated to an increase of 430% to £86,987. Even worse was to come, the figures for 1920-21 were, expenses £88,992 while earnings were only £90,753. At the annual general meeting for that year, shareholders were to learn that the company presently only owned six trawlers. It was made absolutely clear that if those astronomical losses could not be arrested, the company would have to close down its fishing operations.

It is amazing how the fortunes of the fishing industry fluctuate. In the two editions of 18th. and 25th. June 1921 the *Boston Guardian* published this notice, "The Boston Deep Sea Fishing & Ice Co. announce that, because of very low returns, some of their remaining trawlers are to be sold outside this Country". Yet the very next year on the 3rd. June 1922, the same newspaper was reporting that the company had purchased eleven Government trawlers. The prospects of fishing were again encouraging enough for the company to invest in more trawlers and the *Boston Guardian* on 11th. November 1922 was prompted to report thus: "Their fleet will now be the biggest it has ever been in the annals of the company, and certainly the most valuable fleet they have ever had. All the trawlers are new, and are that type of vessel which reached the value of something like £20,000 each during the war, when, of course prices were very high".

The young Fred Parkes, a man of ambition with a shrewd business mind, and a talent for spotting hidden opportunities, was steering the company on a positive course. Benefits from the company's growth were promising, not only to them, but also to the Lincolnshire town, which enjoyed the trade it brought, and employment was most welcome. Fred Parkes was putting Boston, Lincs., as a fishing port, on the map...that is, until an unfortunate incident occurred and, which later was supported by a shortsighted, misguided Boston Corporation.

The incident occurred on 28th. February, 1922 when the steam collier *Lockwood,* a vessel of about 1,000 tons deadweight, under the command of Capt. Thompson, with a crew of seventeen, and carrying 1,500 tons of coal, outward bound for Hamburg, with her steering jammed went aground near Milk House Farm on the River Witham. The Harbour Master of that time asked the Boston company if they could send one of their steam trawlers to assist. The *William Browns* was dispatched down river and after becoming temporarily aground themselves, succeeded in refloating the *Lockwood* which then on a ebbing tide proceeded on her way. However, together with the delay and a severe drop in water level, as she neared the river mouth she again grounded. On the floodtide she was carried stern first across the river and capsized, thus blocking the main channel which remained blocked for five months. Small ships of 500 to 800 tons, by careful management, passing close to the *Lockwood*'s stern on highwater could still use the port, although that was of no consolation to the port in general.

The *Boston Guardian,* on 11th. March 1922 reported, "A spiteful fate has dumped into the river a vessel which, in its capacity as a dam right across the Haven, is practically paralysing the export and import trade of the port". The river banks quickly began to erode and it was feared that thousands of acres of farm land may well be flooded.

Quite a number of salvage companies submitted tenders for the work, but when they learned that it was the Harbour Commissioners condition that the salvage firm take responsibility should the banks be breached, none was prepared to accept. In any case the lowest quotation submitted by Charlton Bros., a salvage firm from Grimsby, exceeded £70,000.

Mr Parkes agreed to do the job for them, on condition the Council met expenses. A report in *Boston Guardian*, on 25th. March 1922 stated that the Harbour Commissioners had entered into a contract to raise the *Lockwood* for the sum of £12,000. It continued: "virtually the actual work of raising the vessel will be performed by the Boston Deep Sea Fishing & Ice Co. After the disaster salvage experts from all over the country came to Boston to view the casualty, all of whom arrived at the conclusion that it would be an extremely difficult undertaking. After negotiations, it was stated that the work could only be done on a basis of several thousand pounds down for the use of gear and tackle, plus a certain sum of money per day. We are told that, the Port Authority, in accepting the contract, have made a very good bargain. The Fishing Company do not profess to be salvage experts, but have taken steps to obtain the best brains in the world behind them. They have also succeeded in securing the services of a man who is supposed to be second to none in the salvage world. It is estimated that the loss to the port weekly in charges and wages is well over £1,000 per week". On the successful completion of the salvage operation, an announcement that the Lockwood had been removed from the fairway was displayed in the window of the offices of the *Boston Guardian*, West Street, Boston on Monday afternoon at about 4pm. The incident however did not pass without tragedy. One young crew member was injured on the day the vessel grounded and another young man, 18 years old Albert Beecham, of Maddison's Row, Skirbeck, Boston was killed during salvage operations.

The S.S. *Lockwood*, was sold by the Commissioners for £650 to Mr. Tom Rounds of Sunderland, who later, sold her on to a German firm for about £2,000, before she was towed to Kiel and broken up.

One would have thought that the local authorities would be jubilant at a successful conclusion of a serious situation and pay for the work done gratefully. However, when Mr. Parkes was forced to present a bill for £12,000 the Harbour Commissioners on behalf of Boston Corporation disputed Mr. Parkes' bill and refused to pay. Their contention was that as he controlled the largest number of ships using the port, he had most to gain from the wreck's removal. Subsequently court proceedings were instituted. It seems to us that the Boston Corporation was so confident of winning, the *Boston Guardian* in their issue of 14th. October 1922, was prompted to write, "We understand that, according to the highest authorities, the Boston Port Authority is in a sound and safe position with regard to the negotiations concerning the S.S. *Lockwood*. It is understood that whatever happens in regard to the removal of the wreck, the ratepayers will not be called upon to make any contribution".

Boston Corporation sought redress for the removal of the *Lockwood* from William France Fenwick & Co. of London, owners of the stricken vessel. France Fenwick refused to pay. He had, quite properly, given notice to his company's underwriters of the vessel's abandonment. Although the notice was good, his underwriters would not accept it. He told Boston Corporation what he had done. After much talking and many legal moves the Boston Company's claim was eventually settled out of court in October, only three months before the case was due to be heard in the High Court, when the Corporation agreed to settle for £10,000.

Fred Parkes was so annoyed and indignant with the Corporation's attitude, he decided to take all his trawlers and move his business, lock, stock and barrel to Fleetwood, where his firm's headquarters remained until his death in 1962, when the head office was moved to Hull by Basil Parkes. The idea of the company leaving the town was most disturbing. Under the blazing headlines of "Boston Dock Sensation", the *Lincolnshire Standard* declared that it was understood that the Boston Company's intention was to move a portion of their steam trawling fleet from the port, Fleetwood, Grimsby or Lowestoft being mentioned as their probable destination. Mr. Parkes was quoted as merely remarking that something was going to happen. It was three weeks later when, in an extremely frank interview, the people of Boston were left in no doubt, as Fred Parkes 'put his cards on the table'. He said,

"We are removing, I expect about half our fleet, for a commencement, at any rate." He continued,

"We are going to Fleetwood. The removal will be piece-meal, and I expect the first boats will be going next week. We shall still be here with our workshops for the time being. We have thirty-eight boats altogether, and we shall be taking about half that

number. Only a little over twenty of them are effective at present. The others are temporarily out of commission.

The position is this briefly: It is common knowledge that the Boston Fishing Company was founded by gentlemen who were interested in the construction of Boston Dock. When they had completed the Dock they then formed the idea that a fishing fleet would materially assist the Dock, and with that aim in view (they) promoted the Boston Fishing Company, and the line on which it was founded - i.e. For the benefit of the town and trade of Boston and the prosperity of the port in particular - are the lines on which it has been worked since its conception, right up to the time of *Lockwood*. That is the main trouble". Mr. Parkes was most decisive in emphasising his comments. He continued: "Without wishing to say anything to prejudice the *Lockwood* case, I may tell you that the position, briefly was this: They instructed us (the Boston Fishing Company) to remove the wreck out of the river. We accomplished the work we took in hand, and when we presented our account for payment we were told that the arrangement was not under seal of the Trust, and the Commissioners would be personally liable to be surcharged if they paid us. We took upon this as a most feeble one, because if they had a desire to come to a friendly and honourable settlement, they could have quickly put the seal of the Trust to the arrangement".

The lawyers involved in this unfortunate conflict had, it appeared, woven such a hopeless tangle of complications, they were perfectly willing to sacrifice the business of the fishing company as a convenient way of satisfying legalities. Now, it seems, the evacuation of the company from Boston had far reaching effects. The London and Great Eastern Railway Company on hearing of the dispute and of Mr. Parkes' reactions, were more than slightly concerned. Their railway was transporting over 50,000 tons of coal per year required for Boston's vessels, which of course was most important to them. One of their leading officials was sent to see Mr. Parkes, and tried extremely hard but unsuccessfully to persuade him not to remove the Boston fleet.

To the other, smaller trawler companies, the present situation had created far reaching problems for them also. Mr. Alfred Stringer, speaking on behalf of the Stringer Steam Trawler Co., said the Boston Company's move meant closing Boston altogether as a viable fishing port. His company would reluctantly be compelled to go elsewhere. A representative of the L.N.E.R., had been in Boston that day, "offering very tempting inducements for the transfer of the whole of the fleet, including

The S.S. Lockwood, lying on her beam end, obstructing the fairway. Photograph courtesy Lincolnshire Library Service.

Leonard Barlow (centre) with a group of young engineering apprentices taken sometime between 1912-1914. Photograph courtesy of Mr. Richard Barlow.

ours, to Fleetwood". Even so by 17th. February 1923, only two pairs of trawlers had left, one to Fleetwood the other to Grimsby.

News was circulated that a large fleet of German trawlers was coming to Boston however this did not materialise, in fact only one or two German trawlers ever arrived to pay a visit to the port. It may well have been they were sent to sound out the situation there. A Mr. Harald Gee came to Boston from Hull, making enquiries on behalf of the German vessels. He arrived in the face of adverse public feeling. Local people expressed very strong resentment at the Germans taking advantage of Boston's facilities and exploiting its markets while hundreds of British trawlers were lying idle. The British fishing industry was also concerned should an invasion of German vessels intrude upon their markets. The *Boston Guardian*, 24th. February 1923, carried the following warning from the Boston Deep Sea Fishing Co.:"If they came to Boston, it would finish the Boston Deep Sea Fishing Co. It is impossible for any English trawler company to compete. They (the Germans) sell their fish for sterling and pay their general expenses, such as wages, in marks. The mark has a much greater internal value. Consequently, when converted from sterling, they are paid a very few coppers a day. That is why, every single trawler owning port, although apparently it is illegal, has taken the whole thing into their own hands and refused to have them. There is no doubt that if the facilities and welcome, which I understand are intended to be given them, are extended to the Germans by interested parties in Boston, Boston will be banned for British trawler landings by the British Trawlers Owners Federation".

It must be borne in mind that, although quite a large number of the Boston company's fleet had gone to Fleetwood, there remained a number of their vessels still operating out of Boston. The thirty-ninth annual meeting of the company in June 1923 revealed that the company had suffered a loss of £10,303. The chairman of that time, Mr. J.M. Simpson, stated that, in his personal opinion, the outlook and chances of making a profit here were almost nothing. Mr. Parkes thought that Boston was one of the cheapest places in the United Kingdom from which to work fishing boats. But, he went on to say, "that was not everything. It was what they realised on the catch that counted". His experience was, he said, "that the larger the market they went to sell their commodity in, the more competition they found, and the better prices they realised. Therefore, any extra cost they might be put to in landing was more than compensated by better prices obtained at those ports. At the same time, he would rather have half a loaf, at Boston, and operate from there,

than a full loaf at any other port. But when they were denied the half loaf, then there was no further interest for himself to be operating in such a port".

Still referring to Boston, the company was experiencing other serious obstacles. They were facing severe difficulties in obtaining houses for their skippers and without first rate skippers, the position was hopeless. By that time, Mr. Parkes had moved most of their vessels to Fleetwood together with some to Grimsby. It seemed that these were going to be their future ports from which to operate.

Mr. Parkes had suffered a great deal of abuse over his takeover bid of the company, but it was the *Lockwood* incident which was the 'last straw that broke the camel's back'. After the settlement by Boson Corporation already referred to, it was hoped the company would return to Boston, but since 1st. April, the beginning of their new financial year, their Grimsby based vessels had made a good profit and for Fleetwood it was said, "We had a rather severe loss at the commencement at Fleetwood, but now we have got settled down, I am pleased to say there is a very marked improvement and we are making progress at the port, quite distinct progress".

Boston town tried hard to recover from the loss of the Boston company. In August 1924, a deputation visited Germany to try to persuade trawler owners to use the port; negotiations broke down however and the effort was abandoned. The final blow to Boston's hope of remaining a viable trawler port came when the Stringer company, the one remaining local concern, closed their trawler operations. The size of their fleet had reduced from eight vessels in 1920 to just three in their final year, two of which, *Elloe* and *Graffoe*, went to Scotland while the third, *Drummer Boy*, went to Grimsby.

It was the end of the line for Boston as a premier fishing port; all that remained was a small insignificant inshore fleet. Boston Corporation in their wisdom, had managed to drive away the company that was to become the world's largest privately owned trawler fleet, never to return. In retrospect a very sad thing for the people of Boston.

From the very beginning of its humble origins, the Boston Deep Sea Fishing & Ice Co. produced some excellent craftsmen. Not least among those was Mr. Leonard Barlow, the son of a local family, who after leaving a local school at the tender age of fourteen years, decided his future was to be in engineering.

Taking advantage of the Boston company's subsidiary interests he joined the company as an engineering apprentice. Unfortunately, by the time of the termination of his seven years apprenticeship, the First World War, which for some time had been looming over the Country like a black depressive cloud, suddenly became a reality. In common with his fellow-men, Leonard went off to fight for King and Country, serving with the Territorial Forces. Unfortunately, he received accidental injuries while with the Horse Artillery and was subsequently discharged.

Having passed his engineering examinations with distinction before the war, he, refused to allow his injuries to interfere and continued his career. For several years he worked for the Whitehead Torpedo Works in Weymouth and later for Ruston Proctor & Co. of Lincoln as an inspector of aero engines.

The Boston company, never slow to recognise ability and drive in a man, always gave every assistance at their disposal. The company's manager during Leonard's apprenticeship was a Mr. Daniel Walker, and both he and their Chief Superintendent Engineer, a Mr. George Palmer, were always most interested to hear of Mr Barlow's success having wholeheartedly recommended his work.

There were also two other young men who distinguished themselves with the Boston company in those early days: two brothers known as Jack and Bill Borton. Both brothers began their careers serving in the engine room branch in the Company's steam trawlers.

The advent of war in 1914 saw most trawlers immediately commandeered for Admiralty service, a large number of which were dispatched to sail out of Great Yarmouth. While serving on board one of those vessels after being pressed into Naval Service, Jack Borton saw much enemy action. During one of those engagements he suffered an injury to his eye. On recovery and after sick leave, Jack failed the strict Naval medical examination due to the eye injury and was subsequently discharged on medical grounds.

Typical of many of his fellow members of the "bulldog breed", he did not allow his injury to interfere with his working life. Joining the Boston company, he sailed first as a fireman, later becoming Second Engineer. On leaving the life at sea to work ashore, Jack started work for another large industry, The Great Northern Railway in their engineering steam shops. He worked for the railway company until 1951, the year of his retirement.

Bill, the other brother, serving in the Boston Company's vessels also qualified as First Engineer, but, after the "Lockwood" dispute" when the Boston Deep Sea Fishing & Ice Co. made its dignified exit from Boston, Bill stayed behind.

For a while he worked for the Alfred Stringer Steam Trawler Co. sailing out of Boston until that company reluctantly were compelled to leave the town to go elsewhere.

TRAWLERS JACK BORTON SAILED IN AS FIREMAN AND ENGINEER:

Bennington BN 9 (Skipper G.N. Gothard),
Wigtoft BN 19 (Skipper J.H. Royal),
Bostonian BN 72 (Skipper G. Price),
Leverton BN 13 (Skipper W. Young),
Carrington BN 51 (Skipper W. Woods),
Salmon BN 41 (Skipper W. Hagnell),
Bostonian BN 74 (Skipper S Melish) and
Holland (Skipper J. M. Barton).

Below is a list of vessels owned by The Boston Deep Sea Fishing & Ice Co. during its early stages, taken from Lloyd's List 1901 -1902.

Angerton	*Bennington*	*Brotherton*	*Carrington*
Conger	*Dolphin*	*Fishtoft*	*Freiston*
Holland	*Kesteven*	*Kirton*	*Leverton*
Lindsey	*Porpoise*	*Revesby*	*Salmon*
Seal	*Shark*	*Skirbeck*	*Sturgeon*
Sutterton	*Walrus*	*Whale*	*Wigtoft*
Witham	*Wyberton*	*Alsatian*	*Bostonian*
Cambrian	*Dalmatian*	*Etruvian*	*Flavian*
Grecian	*Hungarian*	*Indian*	*Julian*

WAR CASUALTIES

During the First World War years between 1914 and 1918, a number of steam trawlers sailing out of Boston were sunk by German U Boats. It would seem that the German attitude to non combatants was more civilised than in the 1939 war because the fishermen were safely taken off before their ships were sank.

Three of the vessels owned by the Boston Deep Sea Fishing & Ice Co. which were sunk by the Germans were the *Kesteven*, *Lindsey* and the *Porpoise*. The issue of the *Lincolnshire Standard*, dated Nov. 22nd. 1914, carried the following report the headlines of which were "To Berlin".

"The men from the steam trawlers, *Kesteven*, *Lindsey* and *Porpoise*, belonging to the Boston Deep Sea Fishing & Co., who were captured by the Germans, have been transferred from Hamburg to Spandau, a suburb of Berlin. Mr. D. Walker, the

Taken on board a Boston trawler in 1905 this photo shows, Jack Borton seated right, with Chief Engineer Mr. Fletcher. The other chap is not known. Photograph courtesy of Mr. Ron Heugh.

Bill Borton, as First Engineer. Photograph courtesy Ron Heugh.

manager of the Company, has received from a friend the following lists of men who are prisoners and the lists have been confirmed by a consul. The lists are as follows:-

KESTEVEN

J.J. Eggers, skipper.
Thomas Baines, mate.
William Rudd, third hand.
William Fletcher, first engineer.
William Harden, second engineer.
John Fletcher, fireman.
Albert Stearn, apprentice.
Harry Robert Foster, apprentice.
Harry Laurence, cook.

LINDSEY

John Dawkins, skipper.
Fred Royal, mate.
Robert Brown, third hand.
Harry Fryatt, engineer.
Alfred Hipkin, second engineer.
George Everitt, fireman.
Thomas Cornford, apprentice.
Charles Smith, apprentice.
J.E. Clark, cook.

PORPOISE

John Smith, skipper.
John Beavers, mate.
J. England, third hand.
A. Clark, engineer.
C. Warsop, second engineer.
W. Blakey, fireman.
William Harris, apprentice.
John Wilmot, apprentice.
John Graham, spare-hand apprentice.

Mr. D. Walker, the manager of the Company, has been informed by the Consul-General in Hamburg that the German Government have promised to maintain interned men from the British fishing vessels at the rate of 2 marks (2s. 6d.) (12p) per day. The owners of the vessels need not now pay the sum of money previously requested. This appears to confirm the postcard from Skipper Eggers to his wife.

GENEROUS TREATMENT

Skipper J.J. Eggers, of the steam trawler *Kesteven*, has sent the following postcard to his wife, which was received on Monday evening:-

"We have moved from Hamburg. I am quite well. I received your letter. Don't send anything, as I am not in need of anything. All my men and myself have been supplied with new suits, new boots and under clothes. Write back postcard...letters are not allowed".

In those early years, the Boston Company fully supported the Fishing Apprentices Home, employing many of the young residents. The Home was situated in what is now a row of three storey houses in South Terrace, Boston, facing the river. It was run by a Mr. Brighty and his wife who was known as 'mother' to the lads.

The boys, mostly orphans, came from orphanages such as Banardos and others. When ashore, they wore a smart nautical 'fore and aft' uniform consisting of, peaked cap, brass buttoned jackets and creased trousers.

Some of the young apprentices were taken prisoner by the Germans during the First World War. Among those taken, who were apprenticed to the Boston company were, Albert Stearns, John Wilmot, Robert Foster, Thomas Cornford, Charlie Smith, John Graham and William "Lizzie" Harris. It was "Lizzie" who wrote most of the letters home for the other boys.

"Lizzie" Harris wrote the following letter to Mr Brighty after his arrival in Germany in 1914:-

"Dear Mr. Brighty and all the boys,

I suppose you missed us when we did not come home. I am pleased to say that both the crews and the apprentices are all safe and well in Germany as prisoners.

We are being treated with every respect, and with the greatest of civility. We have plenty to eat and tobacco is allowed us. There is Stearns, Cornford, Gobo, Titch, Graham, Bronco and "Lizzie" all in one room. We have the crews of the *Lindsey*, *Kesteven*, *Porpoise* and a Grimsby trawler here in Cruxhaven. They have taken to Bronco as one of their own. Each night the boys entertain the others by singing songs until about nine o' clock. We have football in the morning and afternoon for one hour, so you can see we are getting treated well. All the boys wish Jennie many happy returns of the day, and hope she will live to see another 24 years, and we all hope that her son is doing well. Tell 'mother' not to trouble about us as we are faring well. Please write back, and remember us to 'mother', Jennie, Mrs. Horlich, G. Armstrong, Murray Moon, and all the other boys. With very best regards, from your boys, Albert Stearns, John Wilmot, Robert Foster, Thomas Cornford, Charlie Smith, John Graham and "Lizzie" Harris.

We are seven jolly fishing apprentices just captured at sea".

William (Lizzie) Harris, aged 19 years, taken in 1918 on his return from a German prisoner of war camp.

Chapter Two

Fleetwood

On the Southern side of Morecambe Bay where the River Wyre merges with the sea, a local squire of the day, Peter Hesketh Fleetwood founded a small town to which he gave his family name. It was only in 1836 when its first building was completed. In its relatively short history spanning only a little over 150 years, because of the foresight and vision of Peter Hesketh Fleetwood, the new town's expansion was unique. He realised the immense value of its geographical position.

With the advent of the railway and the town's close proximity to the growing Northern industrial towns, Fleetwood's potential was unlimited. It is no surprise, therefore, that it soon emerged as the premier fishing port on the West Coast. It was to that port, another man of great wisdom and vision, Sir Fred Parkes, later moved his trawler fleet after the disgusting behaviour to Mr. Parkes over the *Lockwood* incident. Fleetwood was to prosper further at the expense of Boston (Lincs.) Corporation whose mistake heralded the sad decline of Boston as a major trawler port.

In the 1890's Fleetwood's rapid growth continued as trawlers began arriving from the East and South East and the port became a hive of activity as owners established themselves there. But it was not until early 1923 that the Boston Deep Sea Fishing & Ice Co. made their move to the port. Initially, the Boston Company experienced some teething problems. However with Mr. Parkes at the helm they were soon overcome.

The departure of the Boston Company, who, as the major employer in the Lincolnshire town of their origin, created a dilemma for many of their employees. They were now placed in the difficult situation of deciding whether to accompany the firm to Fleetwood or remain behind to face the bleak prospect of unemployment. Two men who did make the choice of staying with the company were Fred Anderson and Arthur John Lewis. Fred later became Boston's first Fleetwood manager while Arthur soon made skipper going on to be their manager, and later he was appointed to the Board as a Director.

SKIPPER ARTHUR JOHN LEWIS, O.B.E.

Boston has always produced its fair share of excellent seafaring men, and in the early 1900's, when fishing trawlers were Boston's main source of income, the fishing industry was no exception.

Of all the Skippers that was to emerge from that era, the most outstanding has to be Skipper Arthur John Lewis O.B.E.

Born in Boston in 1906 he was the youngest son of a local fishing family. Both his father and grandfather were skippers and his brothers were also fishermen, three of whom were lost at sea during the First World War.

Arthur Lewis began his career in the engine room branch when he joined the old Boston Deep Sea Fishing and Ice Company and first went to sea, sailing from his home port of Boston.

He married his young bride in 1926, about the time of the infamous dispute over the 'Lockwood incident', in which the Boston company was involved with the then Borough Council, after which they removed all their vessels together with the complete business to Fleetwood. Arthur decided his future would best be served by going with the Company to the west coast, which proved to be a very wise choice.

At the age of 24 years he obtained his Skipper's-Ticket, then sailed continuously as skipper out of Fleetwood until 1940. At the beginning of the Second World War, trawlers were obliged to sail in convoy. Because of the threat from submarines, the leading trawler was armed with a 12lb gun and 4 Lewis machine guns. The responsibility for that job fell upon Skipper Lewis, who on more than one occasion was forced to use those guns to fend off submarines.

Then, in May 1940 came the evacuation of Dunkirk. Sailing in the trawler *Evelyn Rose*, Arthur completed his fishing trip to Iceland, arriving in Fleetwood on a Saturday. His catch was landed on the Sunday (most unusual in those days), and he sailed again under sealed orders on Monday carrying exactly the same crew.

On opening his sealed orders, Arthur found he was ordered to sail to Plymouth, where upon arrival his ship was boarded by a young Naval Officer. The Red Ensign was lowered and replaced with a White Ensign. His instructions then were to proceed to Dunkirk to assist in the evacuation.

As they approached the beaches, the *Evelyn Rose,* bombs and shells exploding all around her, was guided to the deeper water by French Fishery Protection vessels stationed a quarter of a mile apart. They were met by troops swimming and being ferried out to the rescue ships. Skipper Lewis took on board 317 troops. Packed like sardines he could take no more and proceeded to Ramsgate, where, immediately after landing his passengers he returned to Dunkirk.

This time he took his vessel alongside the pier which was on fire and burning fiercely at both ends. The pier was swarming with troops of all nationalities who had been fighting the rearguard action. They scrambled on board and so tightly packed were they, it was impossible for them to move or to count them. During his escape from Dunkirk they were savagely attacked by aircraft, 37 of the troops being wounded. Their return voyage to Ramsgate was at a greatly reduced speed due to damage sustained by enemy action. On arrival the ship was beached, the troops taken off and Skipper Lewis was informed he had carried 403 men on that trip.

During the time Arthur's ship was being prepared for mine-sweeping, he stayed with her, but unfortunately he was taken seriously ill with cerebro-spinal meningitis commonly known at that time as the Dunkirk disease. His condition deteriorated, and critically ill, he was on the danger list for over three weeks.

Luckily he recovered, but the illness left him with a defective heart preventing him from service with the Royal Navy. Even so, throughout the war years he continued his career, taking trawlers to sea, building a fine reputation as one of the top skippers.

After the war he sailed from Hull, taking charge of the first new deep water trawler built for 'Boston's' which was delivered shortly after the end of hostilities. On its maiden voyage, the *St. Bartholomew* landed 4,400 ten stone kits of headless fish, grossing for the trip £17,000. What a wonderful figure, even for those days, almost fifty years ago. It was a record which stood for many years.

The Boston Company was not slow to take advantage of his expertise and natural abilities and he was given the job of taking to sea all the Boston fleet's new additions on their maiden voyages and shake-down trips. Although his duty was to find and sort out teething problems, he always returned with a good catch.

In 1947, forced to 'swallow the anchor', his health again deteriorating, he was made manager of the headquarters branch at Fleetwood. Then, in 1951, for his services to the Company he was rewarded by being made a Director of the Board and also a Director of most of their Companies, a Director of the British Trawler Owners Federation and the Fleetwood Trawlers Association. During his time in charge at Fleetwood, he expanded their fleet at a tremendous rate, until they owned one third of all the port's trawler fleet.

For fifteen years he served as Consul, being appointed by both the Danish and French Governments to supervise the welfare of visiting fishermen to the Wyre port. Another little job he managed to fit in was as President, navigation instructor and management of the Fleetwood Sea Cadet Corps.

For his services to French personnel, and his Dunkirk exploits, the French honoured him with the Chevalier de l'Ordre Nationale du Merite Maritime. Later, in 1967, in recognition of a life's work, both nationally and locally he was awarded the O.B.E., in the Queen's Birthday Honours, and on retiring as Danish Vice-Consul in 1976 he was again honoured, this time by the Danish Government who made him, Knight of the Danneborg.

Arthur Lewis and 'Bette', his wife, grew to be part of Fleetwood and the the Boston Company. When he finally retired after fifty years with the firm, it co-incided with their Golden Wedding anniversary. Bette Lewis often remarked that she sometimes wondered if Arthur had married her or the Company.

In spite of his health problems Skipper Lewis survived to celebrate his Diamond wedding in October 1986 soon after which, seriously ill again, he died on Christmas Day 1986. His last wish, that his ashes be scattered at sea, was honoured. On January 22nd. 1987, his family, sailed to Lune Deeps and after a simple service, conducted by Seamen's Mission Superintendent, Richard Underwood, Arthur's ashes were scattered where he had spent so much of his life, at sea.

What a great pity such men as those were forced to leave their home town, it leaves one wondering, "What could they have done for Boston?".

During the period from the 1930's up to the Second World War when this Country was undergoing a depression, many companies, were feeling the strain of the Country's adverse economy. Fishing companies were no exception, some forced into bankruptcy or voluntary liquidation while others amalgamated.

During the War, quite a considerable number of trawlers were again pressed into Admiralty service. They were given the most dangerous tasks of all, minesweeping and escort vessels on Russian convoys, consequently many were lost through enemy action.

On the cessation of hostilities, Boston's in common with other large firms began to rebuild their fleet. The company owned a number of older vessels, many of which were sold abroad, others were simply scrapped, as the firm adopted a policy of replacing old ships with new, a program they continued until the mid seventies when the Iceland disputes signalled the doom of deep sea trawling for Great Britain.

The long duration of the last war provided the more distant fishing grounds with a long period of rest and recuperation. Five or six years when no fish had been taken from those waters had

Skipper Arthur Lewis, at sea, on board the trawler St. Bartholomew. Dressed in the usual fisherman's garb. Photograph courtesy of Mr. Peter O'Conner.

Boston Typhoon, FD 183. Photo courtesy Maritime Photograph Library.

allowed fish stocks to increase considerably while the inshore grounds had been overfished and almost decimated.

Larger trawlers were required, so that advantage of the abundance of fish in those Northern waters could be utilised. In the 1950's, coal burning vessels ceased to be built, being replaced by more efficient oil fired ships. Those new modern trawlers of wonderful shape and distinctive lines were a delightful picture to behold. However those vessels also soon became obsolete with the advent of the diesel engined vessel. For a number of years, both steam and diesel trawlers fished side by side, but as the cost of the heavy oil required by oil burners became prohibitive, steam power was replaced by the diesel engine.

Although some diesel engined trawlers had been built during the war, and had been put through extended trial programmes, they did not prove very successful. Yet in the early 1950's the Boston Deep Sea Fishing & Ice Co. adopted a policy of modernising their middle water fleet with diesel engined vessels. That policy was later extended to the new modern stern trawler.

From the time the Boston company moved to Fleetwood, right up unto its final years, they had over a hundred vessels based in that port. In common with other fishing ports where the company had bases, Grimsby, Hull and Lowestoft, where the company owned subsidiaries, Fleetwood also had its share.

SUBSIDIARIES ACQUIRED IN FLEETWOOD
THE IAGO STEAM TRAWLING COMPANY

The founder of the Iago company was Commander E.D.W. Lawford D.S.O., a Royal Naval officer who had been invalided from the Navy at the end of the First World War.

Commander Lawford's first acquisition was two trawlers from Hellyer Bros., one of them named *Iago* from which the new company took its name. The fleet increased to ten vessels and began their operations out of Milford Haven. Later in 1930, the Commander transferred his fleet to Fleetwood.

A policy of the firm was to develop a family feeling showing great concern if a man left their employment for another company, a rare quality among trawler owners, most of whom, providing there were enough men available to enable their vessels to sail, reflected a cold indifference towards employees' welfare.

The beginning of the Second World War saw all of Iago's fleet of twelve trawlers requisitioned for Admiralty service. Commander Lawford also returned to the Royal Navy with the rank of Captain, where he achieved a distinguished war record commanding Russian Convoys. It was while serving on those horrendous voyages that he won his decoration.

After the War, while many owners were awaiting the return of their requisitioned vessels, Iago added two more trawlers to their fleet, *Red Falcon* (formerly *Cape Barfleur H.213*) in 1954 and *Red Sabre* (formerly *Hargood GY8*) in 1955. Towards the end of the late fifties, the company acquired more vessels, *Captain Riou* (built 1957), *Captain Hardy* (built 1958), *Captain Fremantle*) (built 1959), followed by *Captain Foley* and *Captain Inman*.

It was in 1963 that the news broke of the largest trawler deal in Fleetwood's fishing history, when it was officially announced that an agreement had been reached in principle between Boston Deep Fisheries and Iago for the take-over of the Iago company. A deal which was estimated at the time to have cost the Boston company almost £1,000,000, was by virtue of the retirement at the age of seventy-six of Capt. David Lawford D.S.O. At the time when the Iago Steam Trawling Company ceased to be an independent concern, they owned a fleet of eleven trawlers, employed over 200 fishermen and a shore staff of thirty-five people, together with interests in a ship repairing firm and a wholesale fish business. Iago's vessels fished successfully for the Boston company for many years until they were either sold or scrapped

Five years later, in September 1968, the London registered *Captain Inman* LO 62 together with *Boston Typhoon* FD 183, which had fished very well for the company, were sold to South Africa. Built in 1959 by Cook, Welton & Gemmell of Beverley for middle water fishing, *Boston Typhoon* FD 183 was under the command of the late Skipper Bobby Wright, one of Fleetwood's greatest ever hake fishermen, and the holder of the record for an individual catch of that variety. She was later switched to the Icelandic grounds on the decline of the hake markets. The vessel was the second trawler to bear that name, the first, *Boston Typhoon* FD 272, a steam vessel built in Lowestoft in 1948, was later sold to Norway interests.

Built by Cook, Welton & Gemmell in 1959, *Boston Typhoon FD 183*, seen here being manoeuvred by tugs in Fleetwood Harbour. Photo courtesy Maritime Photo Library.

Another top man was Skipper Bill Bell who, while in command of *Captain Fremantle*, grossed £4379 from a twelve day trip to the West of Ireland grounds when his catch of 456 boxes included 150 of hake.

Captain Foley LO 33 was directed to operate from the Humber, then in March 1972 the vessel was transferred to Grimsby. Re-named and re-registered she became *Boston Tristar* GY 210. Four months later the vessel was again transferred, this time to Lowestoft where she fished for the Boston company for a short time until in July 1976 she was acquired by Colne Shipping, who registered her in that port as LT 327, before renaming her *St. Mark*. Later, she was converted for other work on oil rig duties where she served until 6th. August 1990 when she was in collision with the tug, *Viking Bank* off the North Norfolk coast and sank in 83ft. of water.

Of course, it is not possible to detail all the vessels from the Iago Company, but on page 27 is a list of the vessels at the take-over with brief details.

Boston Defender FD 163. Originally Captain Riou LO 72. Ended her days as the oil rig tender Grampian Defender. Photograph courtesy Ernest Graystone.

Captain Fremantle LO 22, later renamed Boston Attacker. Photograph courtesy Peter Horsley.

Boston Marauder FD 168, seen heen here leaving Fleetwood for the fishing grounds. Originally, the Iago vessel Captain Hardy. Photo courtesy Peter Horsley.

Captain Inman LO 62. Sold to South Africa in August 1968. Photograph courtesy Maritime Photo Library.

IAGO'S FLEET ON TAKEOVER

VESSEL	Reg. No.	Oil/ Diesel	Where Built	Gr. Ton.	Length	Notes
Red Hackle(I)	FD309	S/T	Aberdeen 1950	674	180ft.	Was LO109 Re-reg. FD for the Spithead Review. Scrapped 1968.
Red Rose(I)	LO 85	S/T	Aberdeen 1950	647	180ft.	To Hull as *Lord Howe*. Scrapped in 1968.
Red Crest	LO 34	M/V	Aberdeen 1955	407	138ft.	Sold to Canada in 1963 as *Acadia Crest*.
Red Gauntlet	LO 35	M/V	Aberdeen 1955	407	138ft.	Sold to Canada in 1963 as *Acadia Gull*.
Red Hackle(II)	LO 37	M/V	Aberdeen 1955	407	139ft.	Sold to Canada in 1963 as *Acadia Cormorant*.
Red Rose (II)	LO 36	M/V	Aberdeen 1956	407	138ft.	Became *Boston Invader-O.R.S.V.* in 1975.
Capt. Riou	LO 72	M/V	Aberdeen 1957	391	115ft.	Became *Boston Defender* in 1972.
Capt. Hardy	LO 96	M/V	Aberdeen 1958	448	115ft.	Became *Boston Marauder* in 1972.
Capt.Fremantle	LO 22	M/V	Aberdeen 1959	448	115ft.	Became *Boston Attacker* in 1972.
Capt. Foley	LO 33	M/V	Aberdeen 1960	434	115ft.	To O.R.S.V. RN *St. Mark*. Sank off Cromer after collision Aug. 1990.
Capt. Inman	LO 62	M/V	Aberdeen 1962	437	115ft.	Sold to South Africa August 1968.

KEY

S/T .... *Steam Trawler*
M/V .... *Diesel or Diesel-electric trawlers over 50 gross tons.*
R/N .... *Re-named*
O.R.S.V .... *Oil Rig Support vessel*

Boston Seafire FD 109. She later became a victim of a declining industry and was sold to New Zealand in 1974. Photograph courtesy Peter Horsley.

Owned by Boston's subsidiary, Brixham Trawlers Ltd., the Hawfinch FD 114, later Boston Nimrod. She too ended her days as an oil rig supply vessel. Photograph courtesy Peter Horsley.

THE DUCK BOATS

About three years prior to the Boston company's take over of the Iago firm, they had in 1960 successfully acquired Brixham Trawlers Ltd., (Dugdall & Son), a company which, in its initial stage began in Fleetwood when Messrs. Dugdall & Son bought nine trawlers of the former "Gamecock" fleet. Owned at the time by Kelsall Bos. & Beeching of Hull, the "Gamecock" fleet was laid up in Fleetwood and on offer for sale. The small vessels all displayed the red "Gamecock" emblem on their funnels and Brixham Trawlers decided to adopt the emblem as its own company flag.

Local people referred to those small trawlers affectionately as the Duck Boats, due obviously to the fact all were named after water birds. During their heyday, Brixham Trawlers operated some twelve vessels but by the time it was absorbed within the Boston conglomerate, their fleet had diminished, leaving only two trawlers, *Buzzard* FD 109, a M/V built in Hessle 1956 of 314 gross tons and 127ft. in length which had been re-named *Boston Seafire* in 1961 and later sold to New Zealand. The other was *Hawfinch* FD 114, also a M/V built in Hessle 1956, 315 tons and 127 ft. long, renamed *Boston Nimrod*, later *Glenfinnan* and transferred to oil rig duties. The others had either been sold or scrapped.

THE PURSE SEINE

Built by Cook, Welton & Gemmell, the Boston company launched its latest addition to its fleet. The launching ceremony of the side trawler, *Princess Anne* FD 15, was performed by, Mrs. L. G. Eyles, and children from a Sandringham school who had adopted the vessel were invited to the ceremony.

The new trawler fished as a normal side winder until March 1966 when the company adapted her for experimental purse-seine fishing for herring. As tests commenced the vessel encountered problems, mainly in supplying sufficient power from the main engine to operate the hydraulic net handling gear. They overcame this by installing a Perkins auxiliary diesel engine. Her purse seine net, supplied by the Arctic Norsenet group, was a massive 280 fathoms in length with a width span of 70 fathoms. The crew were trained under expert guidance.

For a thousand years, probably since Roman times, herring have been taken from waters off the East Coast, always relying on the drift net system. For that reason, the Boston company wanted to develop the purse seine, as there is absolutely no comparison between the two methods. For that reason the company, always the perfectionists, took the step of sending Skipper George Draper, a top skipper, and one of the most successful herring fishermen, on a journey to Norway, where he closely studied the techniques of the seine net on-board Norwegian vessels.

On her first commercial trip, the *Princess Anne*, landed 380 crans of herring, earning £2,680, followed by a landing of 187 crans which made £2,045, and on her next trip, 477 crans which returned a grossing of £4,830. Those trips were landed in Lerwick and Aberdeen. The trawler was transferred to Lowestoft in 1967 and her last earnings are covered later, in the Lowestoft Section fleet list. This venture was pioneering but provisionally unsuccessful, partly at least because the vessel was not suitable for that method of fishing. If the venture had been a success, how different the development of the company might have been in the 1970s and beyond!

S.S.A.F.A. FD 155

Named after the charitable Sailors, Soldiers and Airmen's Families Association, the *S.S.A.F.A.* FD 155 was built for the Boston Deep Sea Fishing & Ice Co. by Goole Shipbuilding & Eng. Co. She was considered by many to be a lucky ship; she was indeed lucky when in 1960, while under the command of Skipper Jim Betty, she was the first ever trawler to break the barrier of the £100,000 figure for gross earnings in a single year, by recording a grossing of £100,786 for her one year's catch.

Her luck was tested on January 17th. 1961 when she ran aground at the Island of Coll, West Scotland, where she spent three months fast on a reef and battered by severe gales and seas. Later, after being salvaged she was repaired. In late March 1964, after she had returned to her business of catching fish, she landed the largest catch of hake to be landed in Fleetwood for some considerable time, grossing, £5,886 from a landing of 693 Kits. During the first three months of 1964 she had earned more than £30,000, of which her best grossing for some time had been one of £7,040.

Then the news broke in March 1969 that the *S.S.A.F.A.* had been sold to Canadian interests. However she did not leave immediately. Having been chartered by the Boston company from the new owners, she remained to work out of Fleetwood for several more months before sailing for Canada. Probably her best known skipper was the legendary Walter Holmes who later emigrated to New Zealand.

Compass adjuster seen here on board the Princess Anne FD 15. Photograph courtesy Donald Innes Studio.

A trawler with an unusual name S.S.A.F.A. FD 155, sold to Lowestoft 1975 and re-registered as LT 73. Photograph courtesy P.L.R.S. collection.

When the *S.S.A.F.A.* arrived in Canada, her role was not to be commercially engaged in fishing. She was converted to operate as a research vessel to operate off the coast of British Columbia and the western sector of the Canadian Arctic coast to be used by various industries who were concerned with the utilisation of the sea bed and its associated resources such as oil, mining, fishing and even forestry.

But Fleetwood had not seen the last of *S.S.A.F.A.*, because in 1970 she was back in the hands of the Boston company and again, living up to her image as a top earner, under Skipper Harry Pook. In August 1970, when returning from a trip to Iceland, the skipper decided to try his luck on the Scottish grounds. He landed 823 boxes including 200 of hake and grossing £5,968.

In the early seventies she was sold again, this time to the Hewitt Fishing Co. who sent her to the middle water and Iceland, but in one year she lost so much money owing to crewing problems Hewitts were forced to sell her to the Claridge Group in Lowestoft. This was in August 1975.

THE SMALLER TRAWLER

The smaller class of trawlers owned by the Boston company such as the *St. Bartholomew* FD 27 while fishing Iceland, although they did very well, were never really big enough for Icelandic conditions. Even so, in spite of their size they returned with excellent grossings. Bob Rawcliffe skippered the *St. Bartholomew* for quite a while. Returning from the Icelandic grounds in late May 1964, he made a successful grossing of £7,200 for 900 kits of fish. Later he took charge of another of the company's vessels, the *Boston Monarch* FD 19, also a successful earner. She was built by Cochrane & Sons of Selby in 1955 and was sold to Italy in 1964. The *St. Bartholomew* was from the yard of Cook, Welton & Gemmell of Beverley in 1955, and was sold to Norway in 1964.

One of the Boston company's vessels not as fortunate as the others was the *Margaret Wicks* FD 265. She went aground and was beyond repair. Her skipper at that time was Harry Chandler of Fleetwood who, at the inquiry, was cleared of all charges of negligence. Originally built for Clifton Steam Trawlers at Beverley in 1948, the *Margaret Wicks* was the first oil fired steam trawler to be ordered by any Fleetwood owner.

BOSTON WELLVALE

The story of the *Boston Wellvale FD 209*, is interesting in as much as it illustrates that one man's misfortune is sometimes to another's advantage. Also it is pleasant to learn that sometimes a trawler disaster can happen without loss of life.

Cook, Welton & Gemmell of Beverley, built the 139 feet trawler in 1962. Under Skipper Jack Chard, she worked the middle water grounds before being transferred to Grimsby to fish the distant water grounds.

It was just prior to Christmas 1966 when the *Boston Wellvale* was steaming off North-West Iceland, a snow storm and severe gale erupted and the vessel was forced to run for shelter. Entering the fjord her radar failed and she went ashore off Cape Aranes. Her seventeen man crew were safely taken off by breeches buoy. With the danger of the vessel breaking up and oil from the bunkers polluting the town and a nearby bird sanctuary, the owners and the insurance company decided to sell the stranded vessel.

A local man named Eudmundur Marselliusson offered the equivalent of £150 for the vessel to sell for scrap. He was now faced with the responsibility of moving the stricken vessel. The questions were, would the severe winter storms break her up before she could be salvaged? Would he, the new owner, be lumbered with a claim for compensation following the results of pollution by oil from the ship? Fortunately for him lady luck was on his side, the storms eased and the winter weather was not too severe.

Plans were made for salvaging, and with the assistance of the Icelandic Coast Guard vessel *Albert*, the *Boston Wellvale* was pulled off the rocks at Aranes and towed into harbour. As the slipway was far too small to accommodate the trawler, it was decided to beach her in a shallow area near to the slipway where repairs to her bottom and keel were undertaken. A survey revealed the 139 feet trawler was in reasonable condition and it became evident that it would most probably be more profitable to sell her as a seagoing concern. This proved to be the case as, very soon, interested parties were coming from all parts of Iceland to look over the ship.

Her main engine, a 1,160 h.p. Werkspoor, built under licence by Holmes of Hull, was found to be basically in good shape, and her refit was continued. A new Mercedes-Benz auxiliary engine was installed together with a refrigeration system. New Bridge equipment included a Kelvin Hughes echo sounder, Kelvin Hughes type 68 radar, a Koden Echolot, Sharps auto plot and

St. Bartholomew FD 27. Built in the Beverley yard of Cook, Welton & Gemmell in 1946, sold to Norway in 1956. Photograph courtesy Peter Horsley.

The new Boston Wellvale FD 209, receiving final adjustments in the River Humber before proceeding to Fleetwood. Photograph courtesy Donald Innes Studios.

After running aground and damaged beyond repair the Margaret Wicks FD 265 was scrapped in 1964.
Photograph courtesy P.L.R.S. collection.

Sailor VHF radio telephone type RT 141. The Radio Room was also equipped with a Sailor 65D transmitter and 66T receiver.

Boston Wellvale now renamed *Ran* GK 42, under her relief skipper, Kjartan Ingimunderson, docked in Grimsby, her old port, in January 1972 to land a trip of 1,056 kits, mostly cod and haddock which grossed for her £10,866. Again, in 1975, after the Christmas markets had re-opened, she hit the week's high with a grossing of £41,836 after landing 1,704 kits, 1,600 of which were quality haddock. On that trip the *Ran*, arrived manned only by a skeleton crew, the remainder staying behind in Iceland for a rest. Her relief skipper was, Gestur Sigurdsson. The *Boston Wellvale* come *Ran* had certainly proved a bargain for her buying price of £150.

TWO MORE SOLD

Two more of the Boston company's trawlers were sold in February 1968. The *Boston Hercules* FD 193 went to join her sister ship, *Parkroyd* GY465, which had been sold the previous year. The other was the 426 ton *Boston Britannia*, built at Goole in 1957.('Parkroyd', a very familiar name to me, as it was the name of one of Sir Fred Parkes' early residences, situated in London Road, Boston, Lincolnshire).

Built as the *Winmarleigh* in 1959 by the Vosper yard in Portsmouth, *Boston Hercules*, one of the port's more successful trawlers, was sold to George Craig & Sons Ltd. of Aberdeen to be managed by the North Star Steam Fishing Co. a subsidiary of George Craig & Sons Ltd., to operate from that port. *Parkroyd* was also managed by the same firm.

These two trawlers were later sold to Colne Shipping of Lowestoft. *Boston Hercules* was to become *St. Vincent* LT 123 while the *Parkroyd* was renamed *St. Croix* LT 251.

The other vessel to be sold in 1968 was the very successful trawler, *Boston Britannia*, which had done very well in both home water and the Icelandic grounds. Hewett Fishing Co., Fleetwood, bought the vessel to replace the oil burner *Samuel Hewett*, which had been laid up. She fished for this company for a number of years before being renamed *Kennedy* in 1969, ending her days in Colne's fleet of oil rig support vessels, many of which have now been scrapped.

BOSTON EXPLORER

A personal favourite was the old *Boston Explorer* FD 15, built at Aberdeen in 1965 by Hall & Russell. Her 425 gross register tons was supported by a length of 140 feet. Originally built for the Aberdeen fleet as *Aberdeen Explorer* A765, she was renamed and re-registered on her transfer to Fleetwood, yet another of the 140 feet class which served the Boston company so well on the Icelandic grounds. Perhaps the company was sometimes a little naive, in moving their vessels around so many different ports. Obviously they had their own reasons for doing that, and most of their business acumen was well rewarded.

Boston Explorer fished right up until the end of October 1978, but faced with the troubles of that time, with limited grounds on which to work, together with a number of trips incurring losses, she was laid up. The company tried selling the vessel to undisclosed interests, but, like so many others, she ended up on oil rig duties.

Over the years, the Beverley shipyard of Cook, Welton & Gemmell built and delivered many fine ships, constructed to give good lasting service. One such vessel, *Boston Phantom* FD 252 is still fishing today. Completed in 1965, of 431 gross tonnage and 142 feet long, she was soon in the league of top earners. In 1967, under the command of Skipper Bill Rawcliffe, she was top trawler out of Fleetwood, grossing a yearly figure of £107,425, closely followed by her sister ship the *Boston Kestrel* (Skipper Anthony Buschini) with £105,506. An outstanding year for the Boston company in 1967 when they had no fewer than six vessels at the top. This is shown in the newspaper report reproduced over.

RESULTS FOR THE YEAR BY DIFFERENT CLASSES OF VESSEL WERE AS FOLLOWS:

Distant Water (over 140ft.)

1. *Boston Phantom* (Bill Rawcliffe)	£107,425	Boston Group
2. *Boston Kestrel* (Anthony Buschini)	£105,506	Boston Group
3. *Ella Hewitt* (Victor Buschini)	£ 93,728	Hewett

Distant Water (140ft.)

1. *Aberdeen Explorer* (Harry Dingle)	£100,000	Boston Group
2. *Maretta* (Sid Christy)	£ 98,700	J. Marr
3. *Admiral Burnett* (Bob Rawcliffe)	£ 97,163	Boston Group

Distant Water (130ft.)

1. *Navena* (Charlie Scott)	£ 76,000	J. Marr
2. *Wyre Vanguar*d (T. Watson/A. Barkworth)	£ 73,960	Wyre
3. *Velia* (J. Fraser/G. Wignall)	£ 66,600	J. Marr

Home Water (140ft.)

1. *Arlanda* (Tom Christy)	£ 97,193	J. Marr
2. *Captain Fremantle* (Bill Bridge)	£ 94,778	Boston Group
3. *Edwina* (George Beech, jnr)	£ 85,643	J. Marr

Homewater (130ft.)

1. *Corena* (Bill Taylor)	£ 75,992	J.Marr

Homewater (110ft.)

1. *Boston Hercules* (Bill Cossey)	£ 70,855	Boston Group
2. *Cevic* (Jack MacMillan)	£ 50,000	Cevic

Homewater (100ft.)

1. *Royalist* (Bill Clark)	£ 41,767	Hewett
2. *London Town* (Fred Thompson)	£ 40,820	Hewett

Home water (70ft.)

1. *Forards* (John Banks)	£ 26,905	Ward

Sister ship to the trawler S.S.A.F.A., the Boston Britannia FD 139, was another vessel which was later destined for oil rig work. Photograph courtesy Peter Horsley.

An early picture of the Winmarleigh FD 193, before being renamed Boston Hercules. Photograph courtesy P.L.R.S. collection.

Boston Explorer FD 15, pictured here as the Aberdeen Explorer A 765. Photograph courtesy Peter Horsley.

BOSTON PHANTOM
TESTS DE-ICING SYSTEM

It was in February 1968 when the *Boston Phantom* was chosen to participate in de-icing tests, the experiments being done in conjunction with BTR Industries Ltd. who already were producing de-icing overshoes for wings and tail fins of aircraft.

Rubber tubes, 15ft. long were fitted to the mainstay, compressed air was then pumped in and out of the rubber tubes, and as they continually inflated and deflated the ice was cracked as it formed. It was hoped this would help trawlers to combat the dangerous icing-up of the super-structure which occurred so often in the severe freezing conditions of the Arctic.

Later that year, in October, the *Boston Phantom* was again fishing Iceland; she was by then on full scale trials of the new de-icing equipment. The Icelandic authorities were so keenly interested in the experiments, she was allowed to fish the more lucrative grounds inside the twelve mile limit without fear of arrest. To enable observers from both the U.K. and Iceland to freely board the vessel, it was decided the *Boston Phantom* should fish as closely inshore as possible. Of course, this provided the trawler with access to ever richer grounds.

In January the following year, 1969, as the tests continued, the weather deteriorated, and during a three hour period intensive icing occurred. The new de-icing system was so successful that the *Boston Phantom* was the only trawler able to remain on those grounds in safety. It was emphatically expressed however that the new equipment was not designed with the intentions of enforcing vessels to remain at sea indefinitely in sub-zero conditions, but with safety in mind. It would allow skippers precious hours in which to run for shelter.

Under Skipper Bill Rawcliffe's expertise, the *Boston Phantom* continued to operate successfully right through 1970, and in April of that year, after a trip lasting only thirteen days from leaving port to docking on return, she landed its largest grossing of the year, one of £12,659, followed in May with £10,114 from a fifteen day trip. She had already broken the yearly record of returns for a Fleetwood vessel, set in 1969, but with two trips still in hand, she had, by October taken her yearly returns so far to £128,003 as she attempted to repeat her performances of 1966 and 1967 when she was top ship. Indeed, by the end of the year she was again top vessel.

Her owners decided in the early seventies to transfer her to Grimsby, where under the command of Skipper Walter Nutten after a successful year she grossed £292,970, putting her again at the top of the earnings table for the 140ft. section.

Unfortunately the *Cod Wars* finally ended the trawler's prosperity. In 1977 after three disastrous trips to the Newfoundland grounds by the Boston company's vessels, one of which was the *Boston Phantom*, the trawlers landed heavily in debt. Even so she was given another chance, this time to the Norwegian coast. On arrival on the fishing grounds, seven of the deckhands refused to work, forcing the ship to return home. The men received a fifty six days suspension.

In an effort to keep the vessel at sea, the Boston company decided to try her luck on the Westerlies, off Scotland, fishing mainly for blue ling, but after only three hauls, her crew members demanded a guaranteed settling. When this was refused, the vessel was forced to return to Grimsby. In a matter of less than a year, this was the third time the trawler had been the subject of crew disputes whilst at sea. Soon after that last problem she was laid up.

Early in 1979, the Boston company converted her for oil rig duties, a task she carried out for three years, sailing out of Grimsby until in March 1982, after a company reshuffle, she was transferred, to be based in Lowestoft. Later she was sold to Colne Shipping to continue oil rig duties under her new name of *Colne Phantom*, who in turn again sold the trawler, this time to Carvel Marine. That firm laid her up pending either scrapping or sale. In 1992, she was sold to South African owners and was still fishing at the time of writing.

THE LAST OF THE SIDE-WINDERS

The last of the big side trawlers to be built for the Boston company's Fleetwood fleet was the *Boston Kestrel* FD 256. Messrs. Cook, Welton & Gemmell built her in 1966 in Beverley. Like her sister ship, *Boston Phantom*, her fishing career began very well, becoming the second highest earner at the port in 1967, when, under Skipper Anthony Buschini she grossed £105,506. She continued sailing out of Fleetwood until mid August 1969, when her transfer to Grimsby aroused speculation that the Boston company was withdrawing its fleet from Fleetwood.

Rumours circulating in the port prompted Sir Basil Parkes, Chairman of the Boston Deep Sea Fishing Co., to issue the following statement:

"Although there had been a reduction in the Boston fleet at Fleetwood, this has been part of an overall Group policy.

Boston Phantom FD 252, one of the Boston company's more successful distant water vessels. Later sold to South Africa, last known to be still in service. Photograph courtesy Peter Horsley.

End of an era, the last side winder built for Fleetwood was Boston Kestrel FD 256. She was scrapped in 1993. Photograph courtesy Peter Horsley.

Bostons' would continue to play a leading part in the development of the port. Modern stern trawlers will be the design of vessels required in the next decade. I am quite sure that Fleetwood will get its fair share of whatever we order".

Then, in the issue of *Fishing News*, on 18th. October 1969 this announcement appeared from the company's manager at Fleetwood, Mr. Arthur J. Lewis:

"A further boost to the fortunes of Fleetwood as a major fresh fish port was given when one of the leading trawler owners announced plans for further development of his company's fleet. Mr. Arthur J. Lewis, a director and Fleetwood manager of Boston Deep Sea Fisheries Ltd., speaking at a dinner last Friday night, revealed that his firm were planning to build two stern trawlers for their Fleetwood fleet and that the existing fleet there might possibly be considerably increased in the near future".

Working comfortably, out of Grimsby, the *Boston Kestrel*, fished well for many years, which continued throughout the *Cod Wars*. She was a consistent earner for the company, but unfortunately for her, in common with so many others, problems began to arise.

The fishing industry in 1978 was going through difficult times and in early February of that year, the unique rarity of two distant water vessels landing at Grimsby in the same week did nothing to improve vessels' grossings. Trade, which many fish merchants had lost due to shortage of fish on Grimsby fish market, became all too obvious and the demand for fish at most was only fair. During that period, when the Boston company brought in the only two distant water vessels to land in that week to meet the disappointing response of low markets, it came as a bitter blow. Both the *Belgaum* and *Boston Kestrel* had made long trips to the Norwegian Coast and the White Sea. After a twenty-six days trip the *Boston Kestrel* (Skipper Colin Saunders) made only £30,105 from 866 kits.

By April things seemed to have improved slightly because in the first week of that month, under the command this time of Skipper Ron Stoneman, the *Boston Kestrel*, the only distant water vessel to land at Grimsby, made a reasonable £41,680 from 1,539 kits taken from the Norwegian Coast after a twenty-three days trip.

It soon became apparent the small improvement in fortunes was to be only a passing phase. The sad decline of a once great and proud industry had began. The *Boston Kestrel* became just another casualty, a victim of the Government's weak policy of appeasement. It is beyond the realm of our imagination to understand how anyone can justify, and agree to, a country grabbing and claiming a boundary extending two hundred miles out to sea.

1978 found the *Boston Kestrel* in Lowestoft undergoing conversion for oil rig work. After operating out of Lowestoft in 1982 for the Boston Company she was then sold to Colne Shipping to continue her new role for a few more years before they sold her to Carvel Marine. The vessel was scrapped in 1993.

THE ADVENT OF THE STERN TRAWLER

The new era of stern trawlers for Fleetwood, announced earlier, had arrived. Those vessels which fished from the stern were much more comfortable in which to work. Unlike their predecessors, which towed their gear from the side, hauling their gear involved heavy manual labour, fish had to be gutted on deck in all weathers before being washed and stored below in ice in the fish pound. In these new modern ships their gear was hauled on the stern, all done mechanically, abolishing most of the toil. After the cod end containing the catch was hove up the stern ramp, the fish went below the main deck to be gutted washed and stored, by men working in relative comfort and safe conditions, sheltered from the elements.

Boston Deep Sea Fisheries, as they became known, introduced their first stern trawler to Fleetwood. The *Boston Blenheim* FD 137, built at Hessle in 1971 by Richard Dunston Ltd. Some 141ft in length with a gross registered tons of 517, she was under the command of thirty-three years old Skipper Bill Bridge who on her maiden voyage returned with 1,653 kits to gross £14,239. After her second trip she became the first wet fish trawler to discharge her catch by an automated mechanical system which entered the fishroom via the vessel's only hatch and a conveyor delivered the fish onto the quayside.

Boston Blenheim, carefully designed on the lines of the stern Trawlers which the Boston company had built for the Acadia Fisheries of Canada, was indeed a well built ship. Although never really a top earner, she never-the-less, did very well over the years for the company.

At the end of April 1977 while the vessel was on a trial trip for blue ling, she broke two records when, from the Scottish grounds, she brought home 16,750 stones of blue ling from a 17,810 stones catch, grossing £36,783. That landing was a record grossing for a home water trip ever to be landed at that time in Fleetwood, and beating her own record of £29,032 which she had established earlier that month. As a matter of interest, it was during that same period when the British United's Grimsby based trawler the *Vivaria* on a similar blue ling trip, due to winch problems landed a disastrous 53 kits.

Another similar vessel to the *Boston Blenheim* was the *Boston Beverley* GY 191. She too was a Hessle built ship by Richard Dunston Ltd. in 1971, which for a few years, under the command of top skipper Bob Rawcliffe of Fleetwood, fished from Grimsby before being transferred to Fleetwood. The two identical vessels paired with each other on several trips, fishing for white fish. They also participated in both the Minch mackerel fishery and the Cornish mackerel season.

It was during one of her trips on the Cornish mackerel fishery in early 1979 in Falmouth Bay, when a near disaster struck the *Boston Beverley* almost resulting in her loss. She had been lying alongside the modern East German factory ship *Jungle Welt* discharging her catch, when she suddenly began taking in water so rapidly the vessel was in danger of capsizing. Bob Rawcliffe radioed for assistance when he realised their own pumps could not contain the ingress of water flooding into the 141 ft. vessel.

Falmouth Coastguards, intercepting the emergency call, in turn alerted the local lifeboat and the Fire Brigade. Seven firemen were taken out to the trawler where they set up three emergency pumps. Within minutes, the Royal Naval vessel *H.M.S. Cuxton* also arrived on the scene and stood by while the firemen and the 14 man crew of the trawler worked frantically to clear the water. The *Boston Beverley* had developed a serious list, and, it was only as the water reached the factory deck that the firemen and the crew were able to contain the situation and the vessel gradually began to straighten up. Later, upon investigation, the trouble was found to be caused by a rubber valve which had cracked and allowed water to seep into the hold.

Sadly, barely a month later, both the *Boston Blenheim* and the *Boston Beverley* were put on the market and offered for sale. Mr. H. Hurst, who was Chief Engineer of the *Boston Blenheim*, takes up the story:

"It concerns the final days in this country of two of their vessels, named the *Boston Beverley* and the *Boston Blenheim*. I was taken on as Chief Engineer of the *Boston Blenheim* at Fleetwood in April 1979. In company with the *Boston Beverley* she was at Fleetwood as they were on the market to be sold. They were in fact sold to a Chilean company, Ben Mar Fishing Company of Santiago, Chile.

I was asked if I would like to sign a contract to take the ship down to Chile and work there for a year instructing the Chileans on how to run the ship and also to sail on her fishing trips out there. Therefore, between May and August 1979, we spent the time getting the ship ready for the long journey to South America.

Sailing from Fleetwood in early August we proceeded down to Palmas on the first leg of the journey, then, from there we headed towards the Caribbean and on to the Panama Canal. We sailed together, both ships leaving at the same time and keeping close company for most of the journey south. To enable us to steer a more accurate route to South America we used the newly installed Satellite Navigation Equipment.

Making the journey in easy stages, we arrived after eight weeks in Valparaiso, the main port in Chile, in early October where we spent eight weeks waiting for parts to be flown out from England to repair our engine. Meanwhile, the *Boston Beverley* proceeded to her final destination, the port of Chonchi on the island of Chiloe, Southern Chile.

When we arrived there, just before Christmas, having taken on board a Chilean crew, we immediately proceeded to sea, fishing for skate and other species for sale on the Spanish markets. The fish was transported by road to Santiago and from there flown direct to Spain.

With my wife and family, I stayed in Chile for three years until June 1982, when, due to the recession, the two ships were laid up after the owners had gone into bankruptcy. Later both ships were taken over by the Chilean Navy and we returned home. The last I saw of both ships was when they were in Porto Montt, the southern naval base for Chile. This was at the time of the Falkland crisis".

The last, but by no means least, of the large stern trawlers was the *Boston Stirling* FD 247, one of two identical vessels built for the Boston company by the Goole Ship Building & Repair Co. Ltd. in 1975. Intended for the near, middle and distant water she was constructed to Lloyds classification + 100 A1 Stern trawler, overall length of 124ft. and 389 gross register tons with a fish room capacity of 9,000 cu. ft. Powered by a Mirrlees Blackstone ET SL 16M twin bank diesel engine she had a speed of 13 knots. A well designed wheel-house provided almost 360° vision.

It was disappointing that this trawler arrived when the fishing situation was showing no improvement. The Boston company's arrangement with Iceland soon proved less than generous. The former skipper of *Boston Blenheim*, Skipper Bill Bridge, was given command and under him the ship sailed direct from the builder's yard to the Icelandic fishing grounds. As she had not been granted a Icelandic fishing licence she was forced to work outside the new Icelandic limits of 50 miles. Losing valuable fishing time on her maiden voyage due to a mechanical fault, she was forced to put into the Faroes to sort out her teething troubles. Even so, after a twenty-three days absence she returned with a

Built to a design similar to those built for the Acadia Fisheries of Canada, the Boston Blenheim FD 137 was later sold to Ben Mar Fishing Co. in Santiago. Photograph courtesy Steve Pulfrey.

A typical example of the new stern trawler, the Boston Stirling FD 24, which, unfortunately arrived too late to take advantage of Icelandic waters. Photograph courtesy K.W. Kent.

catch of 1,120 kits, consisting of 580 kits of cod, 170 of coley, 70 of blue ling and 80 reds and although making a grossing of £15,409, on her maiden voyage, she made a heavy loss.

Iceland's policy to refuse the transfer of licences from scrapped vessels to others continued. The *Boston Lightning*, presently laid up, already had her licence revoked for an infringement, but the Icelanders would not entertain an application for her licence to be transferred to the *Boston Stirling*. Therefore she had no alternative but to try her luck on the few remaining grounds outside the fifty mile limit. Questions were asked in Parliament regarding the Icelandic actions and fishing interests including the Boston company became despondent with the British Government's complacent attitude in negotiations with Iceland, allowing the intrusion of outside political influence to give Iceland the upper hand. Soon the Iceland grounds were to be out of bounds to everyone and the *Boston Stirling* was forced to turn her attention to other grounds. The Norwegian Coast and White Sea grounds remained open, but in 1977 those grounds too were getting hammered. The occasional good trip was most welcome when, in March 1977, the *Boston Stirling* returned from the west of Ireland to smash Fleetwood's port middle water record. After only an eleven days trip, Skipper Bill Bridge landed 885 kits, which included, more than 500 of cod and pollock, 200 of haddock, 65 of coley and 10 of dogfish to gross £28,044.

The General Manager at the time, Mr. Dennis Bond, commented on a marvellous trip, saying it was a credit to her skipper and crew. However, later that year prices tumbled dramatically, some of the largest catches getting little in return. The *Boston Stirling* returned from a twenty day trip to the Norwegian Coast with 1,558 ten stone kits which grossed only a disappointing £36,246. Other vessels working further, as far as East Greenland, found it heavy going for little return.

By April 1979, Fleetwood, as a fishing port, in common with Grimsby and Hull were rapidly descending to an all time low, and after Fleetwood Fishing Vessels Owners Association disbanded, it left no-one who could ensure landings at the port. The *Boston Stirling* left Fleetwood to undergo conversion to multi-purpose fishing, when she would be more versatile, able to fish conventionally, pelagically and act as a pair trawler. By October in that year, work was progressing favourably. Conversion, carried out at the Haugesund Slip, Norway, included the fitting of three refrigerated seawater tanks installed in the foreward half of the fish room, the other half being used for wet fish. Also installed were two Hydraulik Brittvaag 19 tons

pull winches, two five tons split gilson winches, and a platform between the legs of the aft gantry to carry the net sounder winch. A hydraulic crane, aft of the bridge was used to handle the RSW tank lids and the Karmoy fish pump. On completion of the conversion, Shiptech Ltd., the Hull firm of Naval architects carried out stability tests on the vessel.

Later the *Boston Stirling* and the *Boston Halifax* paired up and fished comfortably together taking part in the Minch and Cornish mackerel seasons and also pair trawling for white fish. Unfortunately disaster fell upon the *Boston Stirling* when on the 31st. October 1985 she caught fire, ran aground on rocks ten miles from Ullapool on the wast coast of Scotland and was wrecked. She was the last in a line of fine ships built for the Boston's Fleetwood company as, by the early eighties, Fleetwood had no large trawlers operating out of the port.

The era of the Boston company, which began in Boston Lincolnshire, later changing its title to Boston Deep Sea Fisheries was sadly drawing to a conclusion. The company had reigned supreme. Now together with Fleetwood, history had completed a full cycle. Most of the older trawlers had been scrapped or sold while some of the remaining stern trawlers moved to Lowestoft. During that cycle many fine trawlers had come and gone, some lost at sea, and throughout the Boston company, encountering both hard and good times, had done their utmost to develop the port and keep alive the spirit of the town, maintaining employment for men and ships.

Boston Deep Sea Fisheries, now gone, have carved their name in the annals of fishing history, a name which I am sure will never be forgotten. It will always be remembered when men talk of the days when Great Britain boasted the best fishing fleets of all time. As for the late Sir Fred Parkes, Sir Basil Parkes, Fred Parkes jnr, and of course Neil, not forgetting one or two old names of the company, the late Arthur Lewis and Dennis Bond, their names will forever be immortalised in the fishing industry and other places. A wonderful company, from humble beginnings to great achievements, always caring and considerate for their employees, the likes of which we shall never see again.

In this section we have only talked about a small number of vessels which the Boston company owned in Fleetwood. The tables which follow give details of all trawlers owned by the company in that port, together with a smaller list of the vessels managed by the firm for the Adam Steam Fishing Co.

Named after one of the Lincolnshire villages, the Coningsby FD 193 was built at Middlesbrough in 1927. She was later transferred to Granton and renamed James Johnston GN 10. Scrapped in 1955. Photograph courtesy Mark Stopper.

Formerly named Dragon Rouge, the company renamed this vessel after the town of the company's origin in Lincolnshire Bostonian FD 4. Built 1916, she was lost with all hands in January 1938. Photograph courtesy J. Clarkson.

The only trawler of her class to work out of all four major U.K. fishing ports was the Princess Royal FD 176. Photograph courtesy Peter Horsley.

Featured in a video called 'Trawler Boy', the Boston Neptune FD 14, was used to depict life on board a deep sea trawler to promote recruitment of youngsters into the fishing industry. Later transferred to Acadia Fisheries in Canada as Acadia Neptune. Photograph courtesy Peter Horsley.

TRIPS FOR *BOSTON BLENHEIM* 1974				
DATE	**DAYS**	**GROUNDS**	**KITS**	**GROSSING**
18th Jan	18	Iceland	1,141	£30,487
15th Feb	20	"	1,048	£18,010
8th Mar	19	"	1,800	£27,152
29th Mar	18	"	2,160	£26,726
20th April	21	"	1,631	£22,002
10th May	17	"	300	£3,704
31st May	18	"	1,714	£17,764
21st June	16	"	440	£6,802
15th July	22	"	1,600	£25,000
16th Aug	20	"	1,255	£10,006
6th Sept	19	"	2,203	£16,376
4th Oct	22	"	1,461	£18,731
25th Oct	19	"	1,848	£26,779
15th Nov	19	"	1,456	£15,002
13th Dec	22	"	1,439	£20,010
Totals	290	15 trips	21,496	£284,551

COMPLETE LIST OF VESSELS OWNED BY THE BOSTON D.S.F. IN FLEETWOOD

VESSEL	Reg. No.	Oil/ Diesel	Where Built	Gr. Ton.	Length in ft.	Notes
Honora Evelyn (1)	FD 12	s/t	Germany 1912	224	120	Brought to Fleetwood in 1939.
Caldew	FD347	s/t	Middlesbrough 1914	257	130	Formerley *Maristo*. Sank by UBoat Fareos, September 1939.
Admiral Graddock	FD 11	m/v	Selby 1914	295	136	To Fleetwood in 1926. Scrapped 1939.
Maristo	FD347	s/t	Middlesbrough 1914	257	130	R/n *Caldew*. Sunk by U-Boat gunfire Faroes September 1939.
Princess Victoria	FD 50	s/t	Selby 1916	245	124	To Grimsby as GY116.
Bostonian	FD 41	s/t	Middlesbrough 1916	289	130	Formally *Dragon Rouge*. Lost all hands, January 1938.
Revesby	FD400	s/t	Paisley 1917	270	125	Was *Thomas Croften*, sold to Milford Haven. Scrapped 1946.
Thomas Crofton	FD400	s/t	Paisley 1917	270	125	R/n. *Revesby*. To Milford Haven as M28. Scrapped in 1946.
Wellvale	FD140	s/t	Montreal 1917	271	128	Lost with all hands, torpedoed 16th. Sept. 1939.
Cartegena	FD139	s/t	Canada 1917	271	125	To Argentina 1927. Lost on passage to Rio De Janeiro.
Authorpe	FD 91	s/t	Canada 1917	271	128	Sold to France 1938.
Bonthorpe	FD104	s/t	Canada 1917	273	125	Sold to Australia in June 1929.
Lushby	FD 24	s/t	Bo'ness 1917	280	125	Wrecked December 1925.
Passages	FD119	s/t	Canada 1917	273	125	Lost off Jurba Head, Isle Of Man 3rd. December 1931.
San Sebastian	FD126	s/t	Canada 1918	271	125	Wrecked at Islay, Jan. 1937.
Boston Wayfarer	FD110	s/t	Troon 1918	284	125	R/n. *Hilford Consort* in 1955 Scrapped 1955.
Alvis	FD 46	s/t	Ayr 1918	279	125	Formerly H52. Transferred to Fleetwood.
Daily Chronicle	FD 69	s/t	Beverley 1918	281	125	R/n *Commodator*, GN6 in 1934. Scrapped 1954.
Daily Herald	FD101	s/t	South Shields 1918	276	125	To Granton as *Commiles*, returned to Fleetwood as FD285.
Ferrol	FD124	s/t	Canada 1918	271	125	Wrecked on Eye Peninsular, Stornoway, December 1931.
Honora Evelyn (1)	FD165	s/t	Lowestoft 1918	100	87	Formerly *Silhouette*. Wrecked September 1937.
Miningsby	FD 25	s/t	Troon 1918	278	125	To France as *Congre*.
Oseby	FD 33	s/t	Greenock 1918	280	125	Sold to France as *Penfret*.
Seville	FD135	s/t	Canada 1919	271	125	Sold to Australia as *Durraween*.

COMPLETE LIST OF VESSELS OWNED BY THE BOSTON D.S.F. *continued*

VESSEL	Reg. No.	S/T. M/V	Where Built	Gr. Ton.	Length in ft.	Notes
Cobers	FD 3	s/t	Aberdeen 1919	276	125	Sunk by enemy aircraft 1941.
Barbara Robertson	FD 50	s/t	Selby 1919	324	131	Sunk by U-Boat gunfire Hebrides December 1939.
Daily Mirror	FD 71	s/t	Beverley 1919	286	125	To Granton as *Computator,* sunk collision, January 1945.
Daily Express	FD 68	s/t	Beverley 1920	280	125	To Hull in 1933, later Aberdeen. Became *Ben Dearg* FD286.
Ben Dearg	FD286	s/t	Beverley 1920	208	125	Sold to Australia 1954. Formerly *Daily Express.*
Mavis Rose	FD 14	s/t	South Shields 1920	276	125	R/n *Agate.* Lost off Cromer 1941.
Tehana	FD132	s/t	Middlesbrough 1924	333	135	To Grimsby in 1948 as *Satern.*
St. Philip	FD199	s/t	Middlesbrough 1927	301	135	Scrapped in 1955.
Coningsby	FD193	s/t	Middlesbrough 1927	303	135	To Granton as *James Johnson* GN10. Scrapped 1955.
Evalana	FD 55	s/t	Wivenhoe 1929	410	170	R/n *Count* FD89. To Faroes 1955 as *Gareo* m/v. Lost 1978.
Our Mavis	FD 52	s/t	Germany 1929	291	140	To Uruguay in 1936 as *Antares.*
Daily Mail	FD100	s/t	Middlesbrough 1930	386	135	Wrecked North Mull May 1931.
Fotherby	FD262	s/t	Built 1933	397	140	To Israel in 1951. Later to Poland in 1953 as *Pollux.*
Phyllis Rosalie	FD 24	s/t	Middlesbrough 1934	433	140	Requisitioned in 1935 as H.M.T. *Amethyist.* Lost Dec. 1940.
Boston Heron	FD 48	s/t	Selby 1939	314	137	Formerly *Akita.* Early oil fired s/t. Wrecked December 1962.
Julia Brierley	FD103	s/t	Selby 1943	380	147	Formerly *Cardiff Castle.* Scrapped in 1960.
Boston Gannet	FD 30	s/t	Beverley 1945	361	136	Formerly *Aby,* FD138. Scrapped 1963.
St. Bartholomew	FD 27	m/v	Beverley 1946	421	139	To Norway in 1956 as *Bjoena* later *Nautika.*
St. Botolph	FD 31	s/t	Beverley 1946	361	148	Scapped in 1963.
Braconvale	FD 80	m/v	Beverley 1946	299	130	To Norway in 1955 as *Masi.*
Boston Canberra	FD 68	s/t	Beverley 1946	323	130	To Norway as *Gargia.* Scrapped 1970.
Nobel	FD 69	s/t	Beverley 1946	295	129	Sold to Milford Haven, Scrapped 1956.
Boston Typhoon (1)	FD272	s/t	Lowestoft 1948	329	137	To Norway in 1953 as *Rollanes.* Scrapped in 1967.
Margaret Wicks	FD265	s/t	Beverley 1948	366	149	Scrapped 1964, beyond repair after stranding.
Bonnybridge	FD 33	m/v	Hessle 1949	289	130	Sold to Canada in 1951 as *Blue Wave.*

COMPLETE LIST OF VESSELS OWNED BY THE BOSTON D.S.F. *continued*

VESSEL	Reg. No.	S/T. M/V	Where Built	Gr. Ton.	Length in ft.	Notes
Braconglen	FD283	s/t	Lowestoft 1949	338	135	Sold to Ceylon 1950. Sank in Columbo harbour 1971.
Princess Elizabeth	FD213	m/v	Selby 1952	514	140	To Australia in 1954 as *Southern Endeavour*. Scuttled in 1982.
Princess Royal	FD176	m/v	Aberdeen 1952	318	114	Rn. *Boston Lancaster*, then *Corsair*, later *Subsea Corsair*.
Boston Firefly	FD182	m/v	Aberdeen 1953	318	124	R/n *Acadia Seahawk*, Canada. Missing December 1964.
St. Leonard	FD179	m/v	Selby 1953	275	115	To Canada as *Zebra*.
Fleetwood Lady	FD 1	m/v	Selby 1954	370	128	To Canada. Lost 1968.
Princess Anne	FD 15	m/v	Beverley 1955	421	140	R/n. *Boston Wellington* LT740 1971.
Boston Monarch	FD 19	m/v	Selby 1955	466	139	Sold to Italy in 1964 as *Oceania Rosa*.
Boston Neptune	FD 14	m/v	Goole 1955	328	132	Sold to Canada as *Acadia Neptune*.
Prince Philip	FD400	m/v	Aberdeen 1963	442	140	To Grimsby as GY138. Later as O.R.S.V.
Santander	FD138	s/t	Canada 1917	271	125	Sold to Brazil in 1927.
SSAFA	FD155	m/v	Goole 1958	426	138	Transferred to Lowestoft as LT73.
Boston Islander	FD263	m/v	Netherlands 1966	102	100	Former beam trawler converted to side trawler.
Boston Kestrel	FD256	m/v	Beverley 1966	431	142	To Colne Shipping as O.R.S.V. Scrapped by Carver Marine 1993.
Boston Lightning	FD 14	m/v	Aberdeen 1961	391	108	Formerly *Admiral Burnett* trans. to Lowestoft. Sank 1978.
Boston Marauder	FD168	m/v	Aberdeen 1958	448	115	Sold to Panama as *Lina* VI
Boston Phantom	FD252	m/v	Beverley 1965	431	140	Trans. to Colne Shipping as O.R.S.V. Later sold to South Africa Co. Still fishing.
Boston Pionair	FD 96	m/v	Lowestoft 1956	166	103	Lost off Scarborough Feb. 1964.
Boston Seafire	FD109	m/v	Hessle 1956	314	127	To New Zealand in 1974 as *Neptune*.
Boston Seafoam	FD 42	m/v	Hessle 1956	398	138	Trans. to Milford Haven.
Boston Stirling	FD247	m/v	Goole 1975	389	129	Stern trawler re-registered as LO 336. Sank 1985.
Boston Typhoon(2)	FD183	m/v	Beverley 1959	425	140	Sold to South Africa. Scuttled off Robben Island 1978.
Boston Valiant	FD214	s/t	Aberdeen 1946	296	129	To South Africa in 1957. Scrapped in 1967.
Boston Wellvale	FD209	m/v	Beverley 1962	419	140	Wrecked Iceland 1966. Salvaged R/n. *Ran*, Iceland.

COMPLETE LIST OF VESSELS OWNED BY THE BOSTON D.S.F. *continued*

VESSEL	Reg. No.	S/T. M/V	Where Built	Gr. Ton.	Length in ft.	Notes
Lady Stanley	FD125	s/t	South Shields 1917	276	125	To Milford Haven as A543. Scrapped 1960.
Normanby	FD 31	s/t	Middlesbrough 1917	275	125	To Granton as *Astros* EN31.
Boston Attacker	FD 92	s/t	Beverley 1946	333	125	Purchased by Canadian Government for Ceylon 1952.
Boston Defender	FD163	m/v	Aberdeen 1957	391	115	R/n *Grampian Defender* in 1978 O.R.S.V.
Boston Invader	FD161	m/v	Aberdeen 1956	407	138	R/n *Inverlochy*, later *Grampian Loch*. O.R.S.V.
Boston Britannia	FD139	m/v	Goole 1957	426	139	Became *Kennedy* in 1969. Then to Colne Shipping as O.R.S.V.
Boston Crusader	FD208	m/v	Goole 1958	426	139	R/n *Jamaica* in 1977. As O.R.S.V. Ex *Broadwater*.
Boston Hercules	FD193	m/v	Portsmouth 1959	310	115	Formerly *Winmarleigh*. Became *St. Vincent* LT123.
Boston Explorer	FD 15	m/v	Aberdeen 1965	425	139	Formerly *Aberdeen Explorer* to O.R.S.V.
Boston Blenheim	FD137	m/v	Hessle 1971	517	141	Stern trawler. Sold to Chile 1979.

VESSELS JOINTLY OWNED WITH ADAMS S.F. CO.

VESSEL	Reg. No.	S/T. M/V	Where Built	Gr. Ton.	Length in ft.	Notes
Duncan	FD 92	s/t	Selby 1917	324	138	Sold to Poland as *Pokucie*. Scrapped 1959.
Erith	FD 93	s/t	Selby 1917	325	130	Sold to Poland as *Polesie*.
Force	FD100	s/t	Aberdeen 1917	324	135	Sunk by enemy aircraft off Yarmouth, June 1941.
Adam	FD 65	s/t	Selby 1919	324	125	Sold to Poland. Scrapped 1962.
Count	FD 89	s/t	Wivenhoe 1929	410	170	Formerly *Evalana*, FD55. Converted to cargo m/v lost 1978.

Fleetwood Lady FD 1, was sold to Canada where she was lost in 1968. Photograph courtesy of Peter Horsley.

Built in 1958 as the Broadwater FD 208, acquired by Bostons' in 1972 and renamed Boston Crusader. Photograph courtesy Maritime Photograph Library.

Boston Seafoam FD 42. She ended her days out of Lowestoft, the company's last stronghold in the fishing industry. Photograph courtesy Peter Horsley.

Acquired by B.D.F. Co. as Red Crest LO 34, transferred to Canada, re-registered and renamed Acadia Crest. Photograph courtesy Peter Horsley.

Another Iago vessel which came under the Boston flag on take-over was the Red Rose LO 36, later renamed Boston Invader FD 161, ending her days as an oil rig tender. Photograph courtesy Maritime Photo Library.

Chapter Three

Hull

Situated on the Northern bank of the River Humber, Hull is a natural maritime city. Its prosperity depends upon the sea for both commercial shipping and of course fishing, the port everyone associates with deep water trawlers.

When in 1869, the rapidly expanding fishing fleet moved into the newly opened Albert Dock, fishermen were forced to compete for berthing space and dockside facilities, until 1883 when the St. Andrew's Dock was opened for the exclusive use of the fishing industry.

With the advent of steam power, not only did the old sailing smacks become obsolete but the industry became more competitive and costly. The high capital investment required to build new steel vessels resulted in the reduction of hands employed. Instead of the traditional share in the vessel's earnings, men were compelled to accept their position as wage earning employees.

It was fifty-three years after the St. Andrew's dock opened, in 1936 when the Boston company acquired what was to become one of their most important subsidiaries, the St. Andrew's Steam Fishing Company of Hull.

On acquisition, the St. Andrew's Co. consisted of four trawlers, two of which were the modern vessels *St. Just* and *St. John*, one older trawler the *St. Hubert* and a smaller vessel the *Charles Doran*. The company which had been founded in 1897 was soon to become the Boston company's main centre of operations on the east coast. Mr Parkes himself personally took charge. Moving with his family, he resided first in North Ferriby and later in Hessle where a new house was built for him.

The company continued its rapid expansion. New offices were required for the control of the group of companies which the Boston company had taken over. A builder was commissioned to undertake this work. Old property was demolished to provide room for the new offices which were sited on a commanding position at the entrance to St. Andrew's Dock, where they remain to this day, serving as a reminder of a company which became a legend. Mr. Parkes sat on the boards of over forty companies, so it was little wonder the cleaners would often complain about the number of brass plates exhibited outside the offices, which had to be cleaned every day.

In addition to the forty trawlers operating from Hull owned by the Boston company many others were added which had been owned by the companies taken over and many more were under the Company's management

SUBSIDIARY COMPANIES IN HULL

The Eton Fishing Company. Established during the 1939-45 War by fish merchants the Gillard family, it was managed by George Gillard until 1959 when it was sold to the Boston company. Their five trawlers were all named after famous schools which enjoyed close links with the Ocean Steam Trawling Co.

The Marine Steam Fishing Co. Ltd. Founded in 1936 when this company purchased three ships which were named, *Filey Bay*, *Runswick Bay* and *Cayton Bay*, all as their name suggests named after English Bays. Re-organised in 1946 with two ships, but in 1949 *Cayton Bay* was built for them at Beverley. Sold to the Boston subsidiary St. Andrew's Fishing Co. in 1951.

F & T Ross Ltd. The Ross family in Hull were principally shop owners and merchants who also later became ships' chandlers. In the 1930s the firm acquired an interest as trawler owners, operating with a few ships until 1954 when they also fell under the Boston company's flag. Ross had named their vessels after inventors.

West Dock Steam Fishing Co. Ltd., Originally from Ramsgate, the Robins family arrived in Hull with their fishing smacks in the 1880's, eventually progressing into steam trawlers trading as J.H. Robins & Co. Ltd. This company ceased to trade during the 1914-18 War. A new firm, West Dock Steam Fishing Co. Ltd. was formed in 1922 their vessels all being distant water whose names ended with *Wyke*. Their fleet were sold in 1954, half to Boyd Line the others to Lordline. With two trawlers, the Robins family, in 1954 again formed another company under the name of Robins Trawlers Ltd. This company was sold to the Boston Company in 1961.

J.C. Llewellin (Milford Haven) Ltd. This company's trawlers were all managed by Boston Deep Sea Fisheries. All seven vessels were built at Beverley by Cook, Welton & Gemmell in the period between 1926 and 1928. Five of those ships were in the 140ft, class while the other two were 151 ft in length. Their first vessel was scrapped in 1952, the last one 1956.

THE MARINE STEAM FISHING CO. LTD.

VESSEL	Reg. No.	Oil/ Diesel	Where Built	Gr. Ton.	Length	Notes
Thornwick Bay	H241	Coal	Beverley 1936	437	155	To Grimsby in 1954 as *Afridi* Scrapped 1959.
Colwyn Bay	H387	Oil	Beverley 1942	517	182	Scrapped 1964.
Cayton Bay	H72	Oil	Beverley 1949	580	171	Became *Bayella* in 1952. Scrapped 1966.

F.& T. ROSS LTD.

VESSEL	Reg. No.	Oil/ Diesel	Where Built	Gr. Ton.	Length	Notes
Maxim	H164	Coal	Middlesbrough	432	162	Became *Loch Inver* 1948 then r/n *Rossallian* 1948. Scrapped 1957.
Galvani	H 88	Coal	Beverley 1929	353	140	To Fleetwood as *Red Sword*. Returned to Hull 1955 as H80.
Davy	H213	Coal	Beverley 1936	449	161	Became *Cape Barfleur*, 1951. to Fleetwood 1954. Lost 1959
Faraday	H195	Oil	Beverley 1947	538	183	Became *Peter Cheyney* in 1959. Scrapped 1967.
Tesla	H573	Oil	Selby 1948	555	171	Became *Stella Carina* 1955. Scrapped 1967.

ROBINS TRAWLERS LTD.

VESSEL	Reg. No.	Oil/ Diesel	Where Built	Gr. Ton.	Length	Notes
Daystar	H542	Oil	Middlesbrough	558	188	To Fleetwood 1964 scrapped the same year.
Dayspring	H183	Diesel	Selby 1960	414	139	Became *Admiral Nelson* 1962. Became *Princess Royal* 1963. Sold to South Africa 1968.

ALLIANCE STEAM FISHING CO. LTD.

VESSEL	Reg. No.	Oil/ Diesel	Where Built	Gr. Ton.	Length	Notes
Darthema	H214	Diesel	Selby 1929	373	155	Managed by St Andrew's from 1951. Scrapped 1954.

STANDARD SEA FISHING CO.

VESSEL	Reg. No.	Oil/ Diesel	Where Built	Gr. Ton.	Length	Notes
Silanion	H577	Coal	Selby 1930	366	169	Became *White Flower* 1948 owned by C. Taylor and others, managed by St. Andrew's. Scrapped 1954.

J.C. LLEWELLIN (MILFORD HAVEN) LTD.

VESSEL	Reg. No.	Oil/ Diesel	Where Built	Gr. Ton.	Length	Notes
Dalmatia	H474	Coal	Beverley 1926	360	140	Became *Westhawk*. 1948 Scrapped.
Westhope	H590	Coal	Beverley 1927	357	151	Scrapped 1956.
Jennett	H465	Coal	Beverley 1926	357	140	Became *Lord Bann*, 1946 later same year *Westheron*. Scrapped 1952/1953.
Westhaze	H589	Coal	Beverley 1928	357	151	Scrapped 1955.
Westhill	H470	Coal	Beverley 1928	360	140	Scrapped 1952.

ETON FISHING CO. LTD.

VESSEL	Reg. No.	Oil/ Diesel	Where Built	Gr. Ton.	Length	Notes
Reptonian	H363	Coal	Beverley 1933	409	154	To Fleetwood 1952. Scrapped 1959.
Harrovian	H 16	Coal	Selby 1934	422	152	Became *Yorkshire Rose* 1948, to Grimsby 1956 as *Furious*. Scrapped 1959.

The tables above and opposite illustrate the subsidiaries of the Boston company in Hull. With the exception of J.C. Llewellin (Milford Haven), all were owned by the company.

The tables detail specifications of vessels acquired through subsidiaries, from the builders to their final end. It is also worth noting that five of those vessels were 140ft. in length and two others being 151 ft.

Prior to the Second World War, Hull's deep water fleet had developed to the extent of becoming the largest in the United Kingdom. Between fifty and sixty middle water trawlers also operated from there, adding to the importance of the Humber port.

After the war, as with everything else, things began to change. For one thing, fish prices were controlled. Inferior fish landed from the North Norway, Bear Island and White Sea grounds realised the same prices as the better quality North Sea and Faroe cod and haddock. It seemed quality was sacrificed for quantity.

Consequently many of the middle and near water vessels were disposed of, sold to other ports. It would only be in later years, with the advantage of hindsight, when this disastrous fallacy would be seriously realised. The Boston company, together with J. Marr & Son, tried incessantly to maintain a presence of the smaller vessels based there, but their efforts proved futile, the battle was lost. Even so, about a dozen seine

From the Beverley yard of Cook, Welton & Gemmell, the Cayton Bay H72 was built for the Marine Steam Fishing Co. in 1949 and was acquired by the Boston company on take-over of that firm. She was later sold to J. Marr & Son who renamed her Bayella. Photo courtesy Donald Innes Studios.

Another vessel which came with the Marine Steam Fishing Co. was the Colwyn Bay H387. Scrapped in 1964. Photo courtesy Donald Innes Studios.

57

One of the vessels owned by F.& T. Ross Ltd., was the Davy H213. During her service she sailed under three different names, Cape Barfleur in 1951; then on transfer to Fleetwood in 1954, she became Red Falcon. In December 1959 she was lost with all hands off Skerryvore. Photo courtesy Donald Innes Studios.

B.D.F. Co. held a 50% interest in J.C. Llewellin (Milford Haven), who were the owners of Westhaze H589. She was scrapped in 1955. Photo courtesy Donald Innes Studios.

Westhope H590 came under the Boston flag with J.C. Llewellin (Milford Haven). Photo courtesy Donald Innes Studios.

netters of around sixty feet, and owned by Bostons', continued to operate successfully from Hull for some time in the 1950's, until the seine net vessels were moved from St. Andrew's Dock to the Albert Dock where dock and fish landing charges proved so high, the company was forced to sell them to Grimsby interests.

The Boston Deep Sea Fishing & Ice Co. Ltd., as it was originally known, continued to expand. When they were not purchasing trawler companies they were looking at other interests in which to involve themselves. One such company added to their list of subsidiaries was Industrial & Maritime Riggers who specialised in wire splicing, for whom Bostons' invested in a range of new machines. The installation of those machines prompted new business, merchant shipping companies, various engineering firms and most important the Royal Navy, for whom breaking strain for Aircraft Catapult wire had to be tested to 120 tons.

Mr. Jack Grundy was appointed Managing Director. As an apprentice rigger, he joined the Boston company in the early 1930's, serving his apprenticeship under a fine Scandinavian rigger named Haagerson. Mr. Grundy was responsible for the company's take over of the Tyne Wire & Rope Company of South Shields. Although neither Mr. Basil Parkes nor Mr. Grundy ever became directors of the acquired company, they were represented by nominees namely bankers and solicitors. On examination of the Tyne Wire Rope Co. books, it soon became apparent that apart from the Boston Company themselves, Associated Fish and the Ross Group were the next best customers. Mr Basil Parkes, knowing that his competitors would not want to trade with him, decided the takeover must be kept quiet.

The expansion programme of taking over other companies had been a considerable drain on the Boston Group's finances. Capital was required for other developments, so after a while, the Tyne Wire & Rope Co. was sold to Firth Cleveland whose managing director was Charles William Haywood (later Sir Charles), at an agreed price of £450 per share.

An important statement was made by Mr. Basil Parkes during an interview in December 1954 when he announced that the group of companies with whom he was associated had decided on an extensive building programme. He revealed it included sixteen new trawlers now under construction. The value of the large building programme was expected to be in the region of £1,500,000, an extremely high investment in those days for any one firm.

The first of those new vessels, the *Boston Neptune* and *Princess Anne,* were launched in December of the same year and completed early in 1955. Deliveries of more vessels continued throughout 1955, the last trawler expected to be accepted by the owners by early 1956.

To provide for the needs of the Company, the sixteen new vessels were of varied design, six middle water trawlers of up to 139ft. were to go to Fleetwood. Grimsby and Lowestoft each received three near water vessels of 102ft. to 111ft., while the remaining four distant water trawlers of around 180 ft. were destined for Hull.

The orders went to a selection of ship yards, Cook, Welton & Gemmell Ltd. of Beverley, Cochrane & Sons of Selby, Richards Ironworks (later Richards Shipbuilding) of Lowestoft, J. Lewis & Sons Ltd. of Aberdeen, The Goole Shipbuilding Co., Ltd. of Goole and Richard Dunston Ltd. of Hessle. All the ships were powered by diesel engines supplied by Mirrlees, Widdops, Crossleys and Polar, of which twelve were two-stroke and the remaining four were four-stroke.

Ownership was shared by four of the main companies, the Boston Deep Sea Fishing & Ice Co. Ltd., The St. Andrew's Steam Fishing Co. Ltd, The Don Fishing Co. Ltd., and The Great Western Co. Ltd., all headed by Mr. Fred Parkes under the Boston conglomerate.

Although it was Carl Ross of the Ross Group who introduced the diesel engine in fishing vessels, it was Basil Parkes, a keen exponent of diesels, who was behind the instalation of them into the Boston vessels. Indeed, his father, Mr. Fred Parkes, speaking at the Fishing Congress at Pons, in October 1953, said it was his son who had persuaded him to begin conversion to diesel in preference over other forms of propulsion. Basil Parkes was a proponent of diesel over other power sources. He thought the economy of diesels made them propitious for development. Experience had proved that a steam engine would give satisfactory service for up to forty years, whereas a diesel had yet to prove its durability. The Boston company was to announce later that, in their experience so far, they were quite satisfied they had acquired with diesels, a more seaworthy and efficient fishing platform together with an improved comfortable craft than was possible in the older steam powered vessels.

In the design of their new vessels, safety of their crews was paramount and the trawlers had to be capable of weathering the most severe of Atlantic gales. New fish rooms were particularly well designed, insulated all round, well subdivided and shelved, ensuring that fish was kept in first class condition. The forward

Sir Fred Parkes (centre), Sir Basil Parkes (left) and Fred Parkes jnr. (right), leaving the Beverley yard of Cook, Welton & Gemmell after the launching of one of their new vessels. Photo courtesy Neil Parkes.

Princess Anne H268 seen here leaving St. Andrew's Dock in late 1953. In 1954 she was sold to France and renamed St. Just II. She returned to the U.K. in 1967 when she was acquired by another British owner, as Wyre Gleaner. Photo courtesy Donald Innes Studios.

part of ship, being free of accommodation, provided ample storage space forward for all of the ship's gear. Crew accommodation, situated aft and amidships was equipped with internal communication between mess room and crew's quarters and from the engine-room to the wheel-house, another safety factor which meant men had no need to go on deck when changing watches in bad weather either to the wheel-house or engine-room. Another comfortable facility installed was a separate oil-fired heating system for the vessels and crew's quarters.

Always in the forefront to incorporate every possible improvement, the Company was quick to instal all the latest navigational and fishing aids. The latest methods of remote control and telegraphic guidance were supplied by Bloctube Controls Ltd., a great improvement in communications with the engine-room. When installed, this system reduced the risk of losing contact between engine-room and wheel-house.

In August 1961, Basil Parkes returned from a business trip to Ghana where he had presented the case for the St. Andrew's Steam Fishing Co. Ltd., to participate in the development of the deep sea trawling industry for Lagos, Nigeria. In the face of severe competition from the Americans, Japanese and Russians, who especially wanted to train the Ghanians, Basil Parkes returned with an agreement signed in Accra for the St. Andrew's company to provide managers and staff for the six new vessels which were ordered from Seawork Ltd. of London. The company was also involved in training other fishermen in Africa, which they did very successfully.

Two months prior to his return from Ghana, Basil Parkes had been appointed Sheriff of the City of Hull. Basil's father, Sir Fred, his sons Fred, who was Grimsby manager of Boston D.F.Co., and sixteen years old Neil Parkes, in fact three generations of the Parkes family together with Mrs. M.T. Snelling and her husband, were among the crowd which gathered to witness the installation of the new Sheriff in the Council Chamber of Hull Guildhall. Mr Parkes was the first member of the local fishing industry to hold a civic office since the days of the late Mr. H.M. Hanson, a former president of the Hull Fish Merchants' Protection Association.

During the same year, Mr. Basil Parkes had also fitted in a twelve day business trip to Nova Scotia in connection with their Canadian business interests.

The Hull based company of United Towing Ltd., owners of forty-two vessels, was yet another firm to come under the umbrella of the Boston concern. The company was acquired after the tragic loss of its Managing Director, Mr. W.T. Spink, a friend of Mr. Parkes, who let it be known that his company would be interested in buying any shares that the late Mr. Spink had held. During the many telephone conversations with shareholders to whom Mr. Parkes explained his willingness to pay way above the current market price for shares, he soon gained control of the company. A meeting of directors was called, Mr. Parkes was appointed Chairman, and the Managing Director, Mr. Hartley Vertican was later replaced by Basil Parkes' nephew, Tony Wilbraham on his return after running Acadia Fisheries in Canada. Mr Wilbraham went on to become Chairman of the North British Maritime Group of Hull.

Having acquired the shares of United Towing Ltd., which had to be paid for within a week, Mr. Parkes now had to find £430,000. Already over his overdraft limit by half a million pounds, a low limit in value of all the companies' assets, he found the bank a little hesitant, but eventually, after a little reluctance and a stern warning from the bank, Basil Parkes successfully acquired the necessary loan with which to pay for those shares.

United Towing Ltd., with their forty-two tugs continued their day to day duties and during the Iceland disputes when Iceland imposed a 200 mile limit, and the *Cod War* was creating problems they reached their highest esteem when their tugs were sent into Icelandic waters to help protect the British trawler fleet. The *Euroman*, *Statesman* and *Lloydsman* were in the forefront of the action. Much later in 1982 when Mrs Thatcher dispatched that gallant seaborne assault force to repossess the Falklands, three of the company's ocean going tugs, the *Salvageman*, *Yorkshireman* and *Irishman* were among the vessels contracted to the Royal Navy to assist in many different duties for the Senior Service. What a marvellous job they did. On their return, several of the crew were decorated.

BOSTON' ST. ANDREW'S DOCK, DRY SIDE.

Trawler owners, with their very fine looking offices, many of which were built overlooking St. Andrew's Dock, made their home on the Dry side. The Boston company's offices, probably the largest of all, stood proudly at the entrance, next to Lord Line's on the opposite side from where a two minute walk brought one to the next, the offices of J. Marr & Son which today still remain in operation. Engineering shops, net and rope stores, the fish meal factory, each with its own story, are all now gone. Overhead conveyors carried ice straight from the factory to five berths where it was deposited via chutes directly into the trawler's fishroom. Four dockside cranes bunkered the coal burners while oil barges satisfied the need of oil burners and diesels.

After a trawler's catch had been landed for the market she would be towed over to the dry side for replenishment of ice, fuel and fishing gear. Maintenance and repairs had to be completed making her ready for the next trip, during the vessel's brief repose in port, which at the most would be only two to three days.

It would be early in the morning, as the trawler, still lying at the market, her catch of fish displayed ready, waiting for the auction, when a meeting would have taken place between her Skipper, Chief Engineer, the shore gang foreman and the engineering and Ship Repair Company's Manager. Any problems encountered on the last trip would be discussed and all repairs had to be completed before the trawler sailed again. The meeting would have been conducted on board the vessel, thus allowing the owner to visually observe the problems. By 8am, when the repair gangs reported for work, a list of defects had to be agreed upon. The ship would become a hive of activity as dozens of workers of all trades descended upon her. There would be, riveters, welders, boilermakers, blacksmiths, engineers, carpenters, plumbers, electricians, shipwrights, painters, riggers and technicians working in every part of the ship.

All new youngsters just starting their apprenticeship had it firmly impressed upon them, that it was essential they must never leave any sharp edges on their work, as there were no doctors or hospitals available at sea, and trawlermen relied implicitly on the shore men doing a safe and efficient job for them.

After the catch had been sold and the owners had deducted expenses, the trawler's crew would arrive at the company offices and by 10am they would be collecting their settlings at the cashier's window. Perhaps the next thing would be to sign on again for another trip before making a bee line for the nearest public house. The men were only ashore for a very short spell, and probably because the very nature of shipboard life deprived them of the freedom and luxuries which the landsman took for granted they certainly made the most of the little time they had.

I have known men who never went home at all. They would hire a taxi to meet them on the docks, which would remain with them throughout their brief sojourn ashore, taking them from pub to pub and club to club. Of course, the element of time seems to accelerate in happy enjoyable circumstances and when

the time approaches to sail again, sometimes men are a little reluctant to rejoin their ships. It is the task of the ship's husband and his runner to make sure all the crew turn up. Often they would have to tour the city searching in pubs and clubs or even call at men's homes, and if finding a crewman drunk he may take quite a lot of persuading to go to sea. There have been times when a trawler has been delayed until all the crew have been found or replacements recruited while the Skipper awaits anxiously hoping for experienced men.

THE BOBBERS TEAM AND FISH SALESMEN

Although the Boston Deep Sea Fishing Co. did not employ their own 'Bobbers', they were never-the-less important to the company. 'Bobbers' were similar to stevadores, the Fish Dock's own 'Dockers'.

People living close to the Fish Market were constantly aware both day or night of the coming and going of a vast work force. These were the workers who landed the fish from the trawlers who were known generally as 'Bobbers'.

The first of those workers would begin to arrive around midnight. In earlier times it was their job to prepare and rig the lines and pulleys between the trawler's masts which were used to haul the fish from the trawler's fishroom to be landed on the quay.

Between 1am and 1.30am the next gang arrived, they were the labour which actually landed the fish. Landing commenced at 2am under the supervision of a Foreman Bobber employed by the owners. Depending on the quantity of fish to be landed, the number of bobbers allocated to each trawler would normally be six to ten gangs. Each gang consisted of four men who were employed in the fishroom, taking out the ice and sorting fish into different species after which they were placed into baskets.

On deck at the hatch directly above the fishroom another man known as a swinger, working in unison with the winch man, and in a systematic rhythm only perfected by experience, swung the baskets towards the quayside to be taken by a weigher off who emptied the fish into a ten stone kit. This in turn was placed on the scales and the weight checked. A barrow man then wheeled the fish to its place on the market and made it look presentable.

Finally when all the fish had been landed the last gang would arrive to complete the work. They were the Board Scrubbers whose job it was to wash the pound boards which had been neatly stacked on deck until unloading was complete. After a

Teams of Bobbers land fish from the trawler St. Hubert on Hull Fish docks. Photo courtesy Associated British Ports.

St. Andrew's Dock in its heyday, the Prince Philip distinguised by her white wheelhouse can be clearly seen. In the forefront is a Danish type seine netter of which the Boston company owned around forty. Photo courtesy Donald Innes Studios.

thorough cleansing, these pound boards were replaced in the fishroom. By 7am, the trawler's catch would have been unloaded, laid out on the market in blocks of forty kits and arranged according to type and size.

It would be time then for the fish merchants to arrive at around 6am to view the fish prior to the auction, deciding on which they wished to buy later.

7am and the day workers began to filter in, office workers, fish loaders, salesmen, filleters, and carting agents all of whom were employed by the large trawler owners. The Boston company in common with other firms employed their own fish salesmen, who with the booking clerks, did wonderfully well in their dealings with many different buyers in the course of the morning, always trying endlessly to obtain the highest price for their owner's fish. Booking clerks and fish salesmen for Boston's St. Andrew's Steam Fishing Co. were, Stan Denton, Harry Emmerson, Roy Langdale, Stan O'Pray and for the subsidiary F. & T. Ross were, Brian Adams, Terry Pearson and relief man, Roy Stanley.

THE HULL ICE COMPANY

The ice manufacturing factory was opened in 1894 by shareholders, who were mainly people within the fishing industry, such as trawler owners and fish merchants. Sited on the South side of St. Andrew's Dock, it was the largest in Europe producing 1,300 tons of ice per day, most of which went to supply the needs of the industry.

Ice produced in the eight large tank rooms was then moved into four refrigerated storerooms, one of which was at ground level the others above it. Electric lifts and conveyors were the labour saving devices which made storage easy. The top floor of the factory housed the pulverising plants, where supplies for the early morning requirements were completed before 8am when trawlers took on board anything up to 120 tons.

Five overhead conveyors direct from factory to quayside carried the ice from where shutes were used to deliver the ice into the vessel's fishroom. This method of producing and loading never changed, it remained in use until when with the declining number of trawlers requiring ice together with the fleet's return into Albert Dock the factory ceased production in 1978.

BOSTON DEEP SEA FISHERIES
THEIR FLEET AT HULL

Apart from a small number of Danish type anchor seiners, the Boston company's fleet mainly consisted of deep sea trawlers, many of which became record holders and Challenge Shield winners. Four new freezer stern trawlers were also added to their Hull fleet.

The company began its replacement programme after the Second World War and by 1946 they had become the port's premier trawler company.

The policy of the company's naming process in Hull was to be Saints, Royalty, prominent people or the Boston prefix. It is also worthy of note, two or three vessels sometimes bore the same name, although the registration numbers were different and often built probably months or even years apart and at different yards.

The table which follows shows a list of all vessels owned by the company in Hull. It does not include, however, vessels owned by its subsidiaries or managed by them.

HULL

VESSEL	Reg. No.	S/T. M/V	Where Built	Gr. Ton.	Length in ft,	Notes
St. Stephen	H 299	coal	Beverley 1928	355	140.4	Became *Lady Jane* 1949, to Grimsby 1952 as *Recepto*. Scrapped 1956.
Arnold Bennett	H 259	coal	Selby 1930	374	156.2	Scrapped 1955.
Hackness	H 202	coal	Selby 1934	387	152.8	To Fleetwood 1958. Scrapped 1959.
Dunsby	H 306	oil	Middlesbrough 1935	422	157	To Norway 1953 as *Findus I*. Scrapped 1971.
St. Oswald	H 335	coal	Middlesbrough 1935	427	160.3	To Grimsby as *Woolton*. Scrapped 1957.
Colwyn Bay	H 387	oil	Beverley 1942	517	167.7	Scrapped 1964.
St. John	H 254	oil	Beverley 1946	536	166.9	Became *Antony Hope* 1946, to Grimsby 1957 as *Aston Villa*. First oil burning steam trawler. Scrapped 1965.
St. Mark(1)	H 218	oil	Selby 1946	579	177.6	Became *Cape Trafalgar* 1947, later, *Auburn Wyke* 1955. Later, *Arctic Hunter*. Scrapped 1968.
St. Matthew(1)	H 284	oil	Beverley 1946	536	166.9	To Canada 1953, later to Hull 1956 as H70, to Grimsby 1957 as *Wolverhampton Wanderers*, Scrapped 1967.
St. Peter	H 102	oil	Beverley 1946	535	166.9	Scrapped 1965.
Allan Water	H 420	Diesel	Beverley 1946	335	149	To Holland 1953. To Lowestoft 1964 as *St. David*. Scrapped 1980.
St. Botolph	H 188	oil	Beverley 1946	361	148	To Cardiff 1946, to Fleetwood 1958. Scrapped 1963.
St. Crispin (2)	H 86	oil	Beverley 1946	559	170.8	Became *Junella* 1951, later *Farnella* 1961. Scrapped 1966.
St. Crispin (1)	H 399	oil	Beverley 1947	536	166.9	Scrapped 1965.
St. Bartholomew (1)	H 216	oil	Selby 1946	597	177.6	Became *Stella Arcturus* 1946, *Arctic Outlaw* 1967.Scrapped 1968.
St. Chad(1)	H 575	oil	Beverley 1948	689	181.7	Became *Stella Polaris* 1951, later *Ross Polaris* 1965. Scrapped 1968.
Prince Philip	H 32	oil	Beverley 1948	568	170	To Grimsby 1955 as *Hargood*, then Hull 1958 as H170 *Stella Rigel*.
Princess Elizabeth I	GY590	oil	Beverley 1948	568	170.2	Became *St. Ronan* in 1949. Wrecked 12th.Oct. 1952.
Boston Hurricane	H 568	oil	Selby 1948	555	171	Became *Stella Polaris* 1949, later *Cape Crozier* 1951. Scrapped 1965.
Boston Seafire	H 584	oil	Beverley 1948	689	181.7	Became *Cape Tarifa* 1952, later *Ross Tarifa* 1965. Scrapped 1968.
St. Mark(2)	H 520	oil	Aberdeen 1948	613	180.1	Became *Kingston Aquamarine* 1952. Wrecked 1954.
St. Bartholomew(2)	H 516	oil	Aberdeen 1948	613	195.1	Became *Arctic Buccaneer* 1952. Scrapped 1972.

HULL *continued*

VESSEL	Reg. No.	S/T. M/V	Where Built	Gr. Ton.	Length in ft,	Notes
St. Christopher(1)	H 573	oil	Selby 1948	555	170	Became *Tesla* 1949, later *Stella Carina* 1955. Scrapped 1967.
Prince Charles(1)	H 85	oil	Beverley 1949	712	139.4	Became *Cape Duner* in 1951. Then *Ross Duner* in 1965. Scrapped 1968.
Boston Vampire	H 94	oil	Aberdeen 1949	386	150.8	To Canada 1951 as *Zarina*. Scrapped 1969.
St. Hubert (1)	H 104	oil	Aberdeen 1950	725	195.1	Became *Kingston Almandine* 1951. Scrapped 1975.
St. Hubert(2)	H 142	oil	Kiel 1950	568	178.1	Lost 29th. August 1960.
Boston Fury	H 252	Diesel	Aberdeen 1950	386	206.4	To Grimsby 1966 as *Brandur*. Scrapped 1969.
Boston Meteor	H 114	oil	Aberdeen 1950	386	150.8	To Canada 1951 as *Zarbora*. Scrapped 1969.
Lammermuir	H 105	Diesel	Aberdeen 1950	729	190.7	To Faroes 1956 as *Jegvan Elias Thomsen*. Scrapped 1976.
St. Mark (3)	H 152	oil	Kiel 1950	568	180	Scrapped 1965.
Princess Elizabeth 2	H 135	oil	Beverley 1952	810	189.1	Became *Roderigo* 1951. Lost 21st. Jan. 1955.
Princess Elizabeth 3	H 238	Diesel	Selby 1952	514	161.1	To Australia 1959 as *Southern Endeavour*. Sank 1979.
Prince Charles(2)	H 249	Diesel	Selby 1953	514	161.1	Wrecked 23rd Jan. 1955. Refloated and became *Loch Melfort* 1957. To Fleetwood in 1965.
Princess Anne	H 268	Diesel	Beverley 1953	442	169	To France in 1954 as *St. Just II* to Fleetwood 1967 as *Wyre Gleaner*. Scrapped 1976.
St. Chad 2	H 20	Diesel	Beverley 1956	575	165.3	Wrecked 30th. March 1973.
St. Matthew(2)	H 201	oil	Beverley 1957	810	188.8	Became *Macbeth* 1969, Scrapped 1976.
Prince Charles(3)	H 77	Diesel	Beverley 1958	691	180.1	To Grimsby 1976. Scrapped 1978.
St. Christopher(2)	H 88	Diesel	Beverley 1958	603	165.3	To Grimsby 1961, then to South Africa 1971 as *Oratava*. Scrapped 1983.
D.B. Finn	H 332	Diesel	Goole 1961	701	188	Wrecked 1975.
William Wilberforce	H 200	Diesel	Beverley 1959	698	179.9	To Grimsby 1969. Scrapped 1978.
Princess Royal	H 183	Diesel	Selby 1960	453	139.4	To S. Africa 1969. Still Reg.
Admiral Nelson	H 183	Diesel	Selby 1960	453	139.4	Became *Princess Royal* above 1963.

The Third vessel in the Boston Fleet to bear the name of Prince Charles. Photo Courtesy Steve Pulfrey.

D.B. Finn H332. Photo Courtesy Mark Stopper collection.

One of the Boston company's more prominent ships in Hull was the *Prince Charles* H77. Built in the Beverley yard of Cook, Welton & Gemmell in 1958, she was the third Boston vessel to bear that name. During her career she grossed some very fine results. In 1959 under top Skipper B. Wharam, she became third in the challenge for the Silver Cod Trophy, landing 35,707 ten stone kits and grossing £135,640. Although having to take third place which was based on fish landed, her financial returns greatly exceeded either the first or second finalists.

The following year, landing 39,603 ten stone kits, grossing £152,139, she was able to claim the Trophy, but to achieve this, she had spent 346 days at sea. Always presented in the early part of the year, the 1961 Silver Cod Trophy presentation coincided with the 80th. birthday of Sir Fred Parkes, a wonderful double celebration.

A remarkable year for the Boston company was 1960, when their ships were top vessels out of Hull and Fleetwood, with top drifter and second top trawler out of Lowestoft.

Another new ship, arriving from the Goole Shipbuilding & Repair Company's yard in 1961 was the *D.B. Finn*. Built as a distant water trawler of 202 ft. in length, 32ft. beam and a moulded depth of of 16ft, her design included a number of interesting features, not least her modified bulbous bow which gave her a speed of fifteen and half knots. She was also fitted with gallows only on her starboard side. This modification allowed accommodation for a crew of thirty-one to be on the port side main deck.

Skipper Bernard Wharam, previously mentioned as Skipper of the *Prince Charles*, was chosen to command the *D.B. Finn* on her maiden voyage to the Bear Island grounds in early May of that year, returning after eighteen days to gross £12,330 from 3,855 kits, the largest grossing from those grounds for some considerable time.

In 1963 she came third in the Silver Cod challenge, with a yearly grossing of £147,608 from 33,795 kits. She had spent 338 days at sea, a good start to her career. However, six more years was to pass before she again came into prominence, under her regular skipper, George Downs who commanded her for fifteen trips in 1967 incorporating 308 days at sea, when she was again top ship, grossing £141,548 for 31,509 kits.

The *D.B. Finn*, spending Christmas at sea in 1969, with Skipper J. Robson in charge, had no reason for celebrating the festive season, because unfortunately the vessel was, on Boxing Day morning, arrested off the Norwegian Coast by the fishery protection vessel *Norden* and escorted into Hammerfest where

Skipper Robson was accused of illegal fishing. It was alleged by the Commander of the *Norden* that the British vessel was 1,000 metres inside the Norwegian twelve miles limit, and had on board at the time of her arrest, it was stated, a catch of seventy tons of fish. The Boston Company was forced to deposit a guarantee of £5,880 to cover fines and any confiscation of fish which may be imposed, in order to secure her release. She sailed homeward bound for Hull with her catch intact. *The D.B. Finn* had sailed on 10th. December with the intention of fishing the White Sea grounds.

A few years later, on March 21st. 1975, misfortune struck again. The ill-fated vessel ran aground off the south coast of Iceland. After being refloated she was taken into Reykjavic from where she was towed home by an Iclandic tug. Back home in Hull the *D.B. Finn* was drydocked for a damage survey, which found the damage to be far greater than previously anticipated. The estimated cost of repairs outweighed the vessel's insurance value. Therefore on 10th. June 1975 she sailed for Blyth to be scrapped. The trawler together with the *Prince Charles* had been top earners, but the *Prince Charles* was the Boston company's only ship to win the Silver Cod Trophy outright.

For the *D.B. Finn*, the year 1974 began with a reasonably good start, but if we look at the table below of her trips for that year, it will be seen that her fortunes declined over the year, both her catches and grossings declining radically as the year progressed.

Date	Days at sea	Grounds	Kits	Grossing
18th. Jan.	25	White Sea	2,035	£47,357
7th. Feb.	21	Iceland	1,631	£32,213
8th. Mar.	25	Norway Coast	1,958	£25,585
5th. April	24	Norway Coast	2,304	£19,538
26th. July	21	Iceland	2,176	£27,362
6th. Sept.	22	Iceland	1,683	£20,992
25th. Oct.	23	Iceland	1,511	£21,693
22nd. Nov.	21	White Sea	1,851	£17,047

THE FACTORY FREEZER *SIR FRED PARKES*

In a concerted effort to attract much needed foreign currency, Poland in the early 1960's introduced a building programme of very competitive bargain priced ships. Trawler companies, including the Boston Deep Sea Fisheries, were not slow in taking advantage of this financial opportunity to build up their fleets. However, although the *Boston York* and the *Boston Lincoln* were later built there, the order for the company's first factory freezer the *Sir Fred Parkes* went to the yard of a builder who was fast gaining a reputation as builders of stern trawlers. They were of course, Hall, Russell & Co. of Aberdeen. Named after the Chairman of Bostons' Sir Fred Parkes, she incorporated all the latest technical expertise and ability available to the Aberdeen shipyard. The end result was Great Britain's most modern and advanced distant water vessel, built at a price believed to be in the region of £500,000. In comparison, should one be able to find work for a vessel like her today it would cost the owners between £8,000,000 and £10,000,000, the price of the rise of inflation in twenty-seven years.

The *Sir Fred Parkes* successfully completed her trials off the west coast of Scotland under the command of Skipper Bernard Wharam, with Jack Curtis as Mate and the Chief Engineer Harry Skoyles, after which, on the 12th. March 1966 she sailed on her maiden voyage from Stornaway direct to the Labrador and Newfoundland fishing grounds. The duration of her trip was fifty-six days, steaming an estimated 8,000 miles before returning to her home port of Hull to land 516 tonnes of frozen fish on 7th. May 1966. To celebrate the new addition to the Boston fleet, a reception was held for visiting dignitaries and the vessel was put on public display.

Fires on board ships especially below decks are a very fearsome situation in which to find oneself. Acrid smoke and fumes have often claimed lives before the fire ever reaches a man. It was such an incident which occurred on board the *Sir Fred Parkes* on 22nd May 1968. The vessel was alongside in Hull fish dock discharging her catch of 568 tonnes when fire broke out in the officers' saloon. Spreading rapidly, the fire quickly engulfed the whole accommodation area. A man had become trapped in the Chief Engineer's cabin. The dockside crew were evacuated and Hull Fire Brigade were quick to arrive on the scene. After cutting a hole in the side of the superstructure the firemen were able to pull the man clear.

The occasion was unique in as much as it was the first major fire where foam was used. It cost only £200, a mere price to pay for the saving of life, and a trawler worth half a million pounds.

Having extinguished the fire the unloading was resumed and immediately after completion, the Humber St. Andrew's Engineering Co. instituted repairs, work which was to last until 10th. September 1968 when the vessel was again ready for sea.

It was in December 1972, while the *Sir Fred Parkes* was taking on board fuel in Vardo, Norway, she damaged her keel on an underwater obstruction and was towed to Harstad for repairs. The Boston Company, however, decided against this and had the vessel towed home. During the long, slow journey home, they encountered severe gales and at times the Company was most concerned for their vessel's safety but the Norwegians, in common with their British counterparts, are excellent seamen and their sturdy tug eventually delivered the *Sir Fred Parkes,* safely into Hull.

In September 1973, fire again broke out. On that occasion the ship was at sea, fishing on the Bear Island grounds when a fire began in her net store, destroying all but two complete nets. The crew managed to contain the fire themselves, but were forced to put into Honningsvaag for new fishing gear.

By 1977, Arctic fishing grounds available to our fishing fleets were becoming very limited, so the Company always seeking better prospects, after fitting out the vessel for the mackerel season, transferred the *Sir Fred Parkes* to the South West mackerel grounds. A Norsenet mackerel trawl was ordered and a new Wesmar SS220 high frequency sonar working in conjunction with a SS20 model were installed which proved to be extremely effective for locating mackerel. Between 1977-78 a large fleet of about forty freezer and deep sea trawlers from Hull and Grimsby descended on the mackerel grounds, causing supply to outweigh demand.

Despite her many problems, the company's large modern freezer landed many good trips during her time. Regularly putting ashore trips of 5-600 tonnes, and, for an example, total landings in 1969 of 3,443 tonnes.

But by 1982, with little hope for a declining industry she ended her fishing present career and joined the increasing numbers of laid up vessels in Hull docks.

The once pride of Boston's fleet was eventually sold to business associates of the Boston company, Boston Putford Enterprises Ltd., of Lowestoft to be converted for her new role with the oil and gas industry

Boston Putford Enterprises Ltd., later sold her to S.F.P. Atlantic Fisheries Ltd., and renamed *Waveney Warrior* H.39, she returned to the job she was built to do.

SPECIFICATIONS OF *SIR FRED PARKES*

Port of Reg. and Number...H. 385
Official No...308533
Tonnage.......................................Gross Reg..1,737
Net 706

Builder...................................Hall, Russell & Co., Aberdeen
Year Built...1965

Type...Wholefish Freezer

Factory details:
....Fish Hold....27,000 cu. ft.
....Freezers...11 x 12 Station Jackstone
....Froster V.P.
Later..13 x 12 Station Freezers
....after filleting line removed.
Filleting...Baader processing line.
....570 tons capacity.

Engine details:
....Mirrlees National Ltd.
....Type KLSSMR Mk.II.
....2,350 B.H.P.
Speed...13.5 knots.

Launched...9th. December 1966.
Skipper (Maiden voyage) ....Bernard Wharam.
No. of crew...24-31.
Named by. . . . . Mrs. M. Snelling, daughter of
Sir Basil Parkes, grand daughter
of Sir Fred Parkes.

LADY PARKES

The second new factory freezer for the Boston Group, also from the Aberdeen yard of Hall Russell was of course the *Lady Parkes*, H 397, constructed to Lloyds' Special Survey for Class + 100 1 Stern Trawlers and strengthened to specification, Ice Class 3.

As we already know, the Boston company was the innovator of many new ideas or equipment which would be beneficial to the well being of their employees and to efficient production.

With both those things in mind, an interesting experiment was carried out on board the *Lady Parkes*. The increasing amount of work which had to be done on the factory deck, especially in bad weather, had been a problem which the Company had, for quite some time, considered seriously. It is not surprising then, that, in their search for a solution for a stable working platform, an entirely new innovation was tested.

The *Lady Parkes* was fitted with an active stabilisation system by Muirhead Brown which was installed with the full co-operation of the Industrial Development Unit of the White Fish Authority.

A host of the most up to date electronic equipment of that time from the Marconi Marine company was fitted. The new Crusader/Pennant single sideband transmitter and receiver combination, working with an Atlanta general purpose receiver, provided communication facilities on radio telegraphy in the Medium and High Frequency Bands. Other radio and navigation aids included, a Lodestar automatic direction finder, a D-X Navigator Loran Receiver, two Fishgraph recording echo meters with a Fishscope Cathode-ray tube indicator which were designed specifically for fish shoal location and provided both permanent and instantaneous depth recordings. Two Hermes Radar installations with full inter-switching arrangements were fitted, a Redifon GR286 Mk.II VHF, incorporating both international and private channels which permitted the vessel to tune into port and harbour schemes, communicate with other vessels and also transmit direct to the Boston company's head office. To complete the array of ultra sophisticated electronics, a Decca Navigator Mk.XII and Decca Navigator Marine Automatic Plotter were also included.

Well-appointed quarters for the Skipper were complemented by eight single officers' cabins, and six by four berth cabins provided comfortable accommodation for the rest of the crew. Luxurious amenities, unbelievable only a few short years before, now included showers, toilets, a laundry with electric washing machines and a drying room. An off-duty recreation room was there for the enjoyment of the crew, while a large well equipped galley turned out meals cooked on a 2KS6 electric cooker made strangely enough, by Kempsafe Oil Burners Ltd. The internal heating and ventilation system by Norris Warming Co. Ltd. maintained a cabin temperature of 70°F. A far cry from the primitive arrangements, or the absence of them, of the old days.

Appointed to command the new ship was Skipper Peter Craven, who had been with the company since the mid 1960's taking charge of his first ship as skipper in 1961 when he soon

Sir Fred Parkes H385.
Photo courtesy Peter
Horsley.

Lady Parkes H397. Photo
courtesy J.K. Byass.

made a name as a top man and for a time was the youngest skipper sailing out of Hull.

Sailing direct from Aberdeen on the 18th. May 1966, Skipper Craven took the *Lady Parkes* on her maiden voyage to the N.E. Canadian grounds. Fishing was slack on the Labrador and Newfoundland grounds and the new trawler was forced to steam an estimated 12,000 miles before completing her trip and returning home. Arriving for the first time at her home port of Hull on the 25th. July 1966 after a sixty-eight days at sea to land 543 tonnes of cod and codling. Her catch was also the first to be unloaded by automatic conveyor system.

Leaving Hull on the 4th. August 1966 the *Lady Parkes* began her second trip, returning to the N.E. Atlantic Labrador and Greenland grounds. Travelling among the ice flows she sustained some damage below the water line. Fortunately, the watertight bulkhead and her pumps contained the ingress of water enabling her to complete a sixty-seven days trip to land in Hull, 502 tonnes of wholefish and fifteen tonnes of fillets, before undertaking dry docking and repairs.

She was top British Freezer in 1968 after landing 3,790 tonnes and again in 1969 when she landed a record catch for the year of 4,169 tonnes from seven trips and 288 days at sea, of which Skipper Peter Craven completed six and Skipper Paddy Donoghue one trip.

1977 saw the *Lady Parkes* sold to French owners for conversion to a research vessel in preparation for her new role working in the Antarctic as a geophysical, seismographic research vessel for shore installations.

SPECIFICATIONS OF *LADY PARKES*

Port of Reg. and Number...H. 397
Official No..308543
Tonnage..Gross Reg..1,746
                                                                    Net 690

Builder....................................Hall, Russell & Co., Aberdeen
Year Built..1966

Type...Wholefish Freezer

Factory details:
....Fish Hold...27,000 cu. ft.
....Freezers...11 x 12 Station Jackstone
....Froster V.P.
Later..13 x 12 Station Freezers
....after filleting line removed.
Filleting ....Baader processing line.
....570 tons capacity.

Engine details:
....Mirrlees National Ltd.
....Type KLSSMR Mk.II.
....2,350 B.H.P.
Speed..13.5 knots.

Launched....................................22nd. February 1966.
Skipper (Maiden voyage) ....Peter Craven.
No. of crew..24-31.
Named by ....Mrs. J. Ingle, Grand-daughter of
                                                            of Sir Fred Parkes.

A 'MAYDAY' CALL

It was just after midnight on the 8th. December 1964, when the trawler, *St. Matthew* (Skipper Craven), intercepted a 'Mayday call' which is the International Code signal for ships in distress. The urgent message had been sent by another trawler, the *Arctic Adventurer*. A boiler had burst in the engineroom, and more, the Chief Engineer, the Second Engineer and the Firemen had received severe injuries from which they had later died.

The stricken vessel was at the time 150 miles from the nearest land, battling against a force 8/9 gale en route for the White Sea grounds. Now, in total darkness, without lights because of a power failure she had been forced to transmit her 'Mayday' on a battery powered radio set. Helpless and at the mercy of the cruel, violent, stormy North Sea her only hope was for someone to come to her aid.

Skipper Craven, in his first command, immediately altered course and headed for the casualty. The vessel was sighted at 5am but the atrocious weather and early morning darkness prevented any attempt to get a tow on board the *Arctic Adventurer*.

As dawn broke, in the grey glimmer of morning light, the *St. Matthew* fired all her three rockets. Unfortunately, in the gale force wind, two fell short and the third went wide. It all depended now on the four rockets on board the *Arctic Adventurer*. She fired off her first one, the aim was accurate, it sped across the *St. Matthew* but alas the line broke, her second one also broke and her third fell short. All hope now rested upon the last rocket. Like the first rocket, it made a bee line directly for the *St. Matthew*. This time however the line held, the crew were able to haul in the line taking the tow line on board. With the tow rope now safely secured, the long, slow journey home began. As the day progressed, the weather improved. With decreasing wind and a sea more calm, the *St. Matthew* was able to increase her speed to seven knots.

Off Flamborough Head, Skipper Craven passed the tow to the Hull tug *Workman* leaving him free to return to Hull to prepare his ship and resume his trip to the fishing grounds.

UNDER ARREST

The second trawler to bear the name of *St. Matthew* had the registered number H 201, a vessel of 810 g.r.t. and also owned by the Boston company.

On one particular day in October 1967, the Icelandic Authorities issued a statement to the effect that, the *St. Matthew*, (Skipper Robert Ford of Hessle) had been arrested in Icelandic waters, and escorted into Seydisfjoruder following a sea chase during which the Icelandic gunboat *Thor* had fired several shots at the vessel.

It would appear the skipper of the *St. Matthew*, had refused to stop his ship until the Commanding Officer of the *Thor* had threatened to sink his vessel. The Skipper was summoned to court on a charge of fishing inside Icelandic limits.

At the time the Boston Deep Sea Fishing Co. knew nothing of the incident. Their only knowledge came from press reports from Reykjavic. Although this incident happened before Iceland's audacious demands for extensive limits which led to the Cod Wars, they were always temperamental in their regard to fishing limits, often imposing inflated fines.

This second *St. Matthew* (H201), sailed on 28th. March 1969. It was to be her final trip under the Boston flag, on her return she was subsequently sold.

During the Boston company's trading years, they bought and sold an extremely large number of trawlers. Many fine ships came and went. So it was, in August 1968, as the company took delivery of its third new freezer trawler, the *Boston York*, another old lady of the sea, the *Princess Royal*, was in the process of being sold to South African owners. After undergoing her final survey on Grimsby slipway, she left for her new home port.

The *Princess Royal*, was the only trawler of her class to operate from all four of the major fishing ports in the U.K. Since she entered service in 1961, she had fished out of Hull, Fleetwood, Aberdeen and Grimsby. In Hull and Fleetwood as the *Dayspring*, Aberdeen as the *Admiral Nelson* while in Grimsby she was known as the *Princess Royal*.

BOSTON YORK

Constructed at the Gdynia shipyard in Poland, the *Boston York*, was one of four trawlers of similar design, all of which were built in Poland, to Lloyds Class + 100 Stern Trawler, and specially strengthened against ice.

Besides Skipper George Downs, those accompanying her on her delivery trip from Gdynia were Mr. Neil Parkes, Mr. J Bayram, (the group's technical director) and Mr. M. McInnes of Grimsby who was one of the company's managers.

The *Boston York* invited widespread local interest in Hull, her design the subject of much favourable comment.

The first trawler to be named St. Matthew H284 was sold to Consolidated Fisheries in 1957 and carried the longest name of any Grimsby Trawler when she was renamed Wolverhampton Wanderers GY31. The second St. Matthew, was registered H201. Photo courtesy Donald Innes Studios.

The first all freezer trawler built in Poland for any British owner was the Boston York H3, seen here brought up at anchor in the Humber. Photo courtesy J.K. Byass.

Skipper Downs first sailed for the Boston company in 1949 and over the years he had achieved an outstanding record of service to the company. As the top skipper of the Hull trawler *D.B. Finn*, he grossed top returns for any conventional British trawler, when in 1967 his returns for the year realised £150,000. For that admirable accomplishment a presentation of a silver tea service was made to him, inscribed to mark the occasion.

It came as no surprise therefore when he was offered the appointment of skipper of the *Boston York*.

A spacious wheelhouse of the popular T-shape design incorporated a radio room on the port side and a chart room on the starboard. No expense was spared in the provision of all the latest modern equipment available which was compactly installed. A central console unit housed fish finding and navigation equipment, two Kelvin Hughes 19/9 radars of which one was compass stabilised, a Decca Navigator, Sperry Autopilot and gyro compass, a Kelvin Hughes MS29 Echo Sounder and a Redifon SRE 103 intercom, broadcast-public address system. A Koden KS500 Automatic Direction Finder, a Koden LC-1 Loran and a full communications system by Redifon, comprising a main G341 DSB/SSB 1200 watt transmitter/receiver and a GR286 mk.3 VHF completed the vast myriad of installations.

Although somewhat smaller than other freezer trawlers, the *Boston York's* operation capacity apart from carrying capacity was equal to its larger counterparts. Her fuel bunkers stored 370 tons of oil while fresh water tanks held 40 tons, and cargo capacity was 350 to 400 tons of frozen fish. Another innovation was the introduction of traversing towing blocks, a provision facilitating a system of shooting and hauling gear, which minimised the need for manual handling of wires, most advantageous when in icy conditions.

Five Jackstone Froster vertical plate freezers with a total daily output of about 30 tons of blocks of frozen fish were installed on her factory deck which was situated below the main trawl deck. Designed with comfort, efficiency and production in mind, the catch was emptied through the upper entry hatch on the trawl deck, passing down onto the working table, located traversely just forward of the shute. Here the fish were gutted, placed on a conveyor and delivered to the washer. Offal was discharged directly overboard via another conveyor. Sheltered from the weather, the crew carried all this work out in the comfort of between decks.

The *Boston York*, (Skipper George Downs) sailed on her maiden voyage from Hull to the White Sea on 18th. July 1968, returning after thirty-two days to land 350 tonnes of frozen fish, almost a full capacity stowage.

There were times when crew-members became totally disillusioned with the tedious life on board trawlers and it is not unknown for men at times, in attempting to delay sailing, to sabotage vessels. On one particular day in September 1971, the *Boston York* was outward bound for the fishing grounds when four fires were intentionally ignited by a crew member. Fortunately for the ship and the remainder of the crew, the fires were detected by the vessel's own fire detection system and dealt with accordingly. The skipper at the time, Ray Richardson, put into Aberdeen where the person responsible was removed by the police.

SPECIFICATIONS OF *BOSTON YORK*

Port of Reg. and Number . . . . .H. 3
Official No 334087
Tonnage . . . . .Gross Reg. 846
Net 285

Builder . . . . .Stocznia Im Komuny
Year Built 1967

Type . . . . .Wholefish Freezer

Factory details:
. . . . .Fish Hold...21,200 cu. ft.
. . . . .Freezers....5 Jackstone Froster V.P.Freezers
. . . . .5 X 20 Station Freezers capable
. . . . .output 30 Tons per day.
Engine details:
. . . . .Mirrlees National Ltd.
. . . . .Type KLSSMR 8.
. . . . .2,500 B.H.P.
Speed . . . . .15.5 knots.

Launched . . . . .31st. January 1968.
Skipper (Maiden voyage) . . . . .George Downs.
No. of crew . . . . .22-28.
Named by . . . . .Izabella Ereczanik, Journalist
. . . . .with the local newspaper
. . . . .Go's Wybrzeia.

PRINCESS ANNE

Last of the large freezer trawlers built for the Boston company, the *Princess Anne* was the first British trawler constructed to Lloyds' Class 1 Ice Specification. Strengthened to this standard by closer frame spacing and heavy gauge steel hull enabled her to compete with Russian and German fleets working the ice-packed Labrador grounds. Her design also incorporated the ability to fish anywhere from the Arctic to the Antarctic.

She had been ordered in 1971 from Gregson's Shipyard in Blyth, and scheduled for delivery in 1973, but only the hull had been built when the firm went out of business. Swan Hunter the Cleveland shipyard took over the vessel's completion. It was therefore not until 8th. October 1974, three years after the initial order, that the *Princess Anne* was able to sail on her maiden voyage from Hull.

Built on the now familiar lines of the *Sir Fred Parkes* and *Lady Parkes*, the new vessel was capable of trawling well below 500 fathoms. She also had installed a net drum which neatly housed one of the largest German Engel pelagic trawls. Her accommodation included a hospital space, single cabins and saloon for officers and double cabins and messdeck for crew-members. The skipper enjoyed the comfort of his own dayroom, bedroom and bathroom.

She was the second of Boston's vessels with that name. The first was built in 1955, a 140ft. side trawler, but was out of service by the time the new vessel arrived.

Skipper Peter Craven took the *Princess Anne* to the White Sea grounds on her first trip, leaving Hull on the 8th. October 1974. After eleven weeks at sea she returned just before Christmas to find a strike by the maintenance and repair workers had forced the landing facilities to become idle. Although the stoppage ended by late December, by then eleven freezer trawlers were waiting to land. When her turn finally came she put ashore 664 tonnes, mainly cod.

To the White Sea again for her third trip, the ship encountered atrocious weather. Heavy daily snowfalls produced bad visibility and yet on her return she was able to land another record catch of 779 tonnes, beating Thomas Hamling & Co's. *St Benedict*, which had held the record for only twelve days with a catch off 755 tonnes for a seventy days trip to the White Sea and Bear Island. The *Princess Anne's* best haul on her trip had been 450 baskets and fishing was said to be very patchy. This record breaking achievement was celebrated by a champagne party at the Boston company's offices attended by Mr. Neil Parkes and Hull manager Mr. Angus Scotland.

There was one occasion when in December 1975 the vessel's stability was tested to the full. While steaming home from the Newfoundland grounds, a savage storm blew up. With wind abaft the beam, running full speed before a following sea, she suddenly dropped off the crest of a large wave careering hastily down the wall of water and hitting the the deep trough with such tremendous impact, causing a fractured sea water pipe and putting one engine completely out of action. One of the ship's engineers described the effect as, "like dropping down a fast lift and then thrown off your feet by the impact, which blacked out the ship and displacing many of the engine-room gratings". Only the fact that, together with the extra strong construction of the vessel, and the other engine not damaged allowed the ship to maintain steerage way.

The *Princess Anne* had sustained some damage and after returning to Newfoundland where she put into St. Johns for repairs, she arrived in Hull, docking on Christmas Day.

One of the vessels chosen to represent the fishing fleet in the 1977 Queen's Jubilee Spithead Review, she returned from the fishing grounds, steaming directly into Hull for stores before going onto Spithead for five days, with her catch intact, stored in the freezer rooms which had the ability to maintain fish in good condition for over a year.

Ever increasing pressure on the Northern fishing grounds and small quotas forced the *Princess Anne* to turn to mackerel fishing. The Boston company tried hard to keep her fishing all year but small quotas proved far from economic, so much so that on 13th. November 1981, Skipper Craven sailed her to Bergen, Norway, to be converted into a survey ship

SPECIFICATIONS OF *PRINCESS ANNE*

Port of Reg. and Number...H. 269
Official No 362252
Tonnage.......................................Gross Reg..1,476
Net 541

Builder ....Gregson & Co., Ltd. Blyth. and
....Cleland S.B. Co., Ltd. Wallsend.
Year Built..1974

Type...Wholefish Freezer

Princess Anne H269. Photo Courtesy Donald Innes Studios.

Factory details:

....Fish Hold...800 Tons capacity.
...................................Freezers....2 banks of 11 x 12 Station
....Jackstone Froster V.P.
Output ....50 tons per day
....650 cu.ft. Halibut room.
...................................Baader Type 166 Gutting machine

Engine details:

....Mirrlees Blackstone.
....2 x Type KLSSMR Mk.II.
....2 x 1,800 B.H.P.
Speed...16 knots.

Launched..15th. May 1973.
Skipper (Maiden voyage) ....Peter Craven.
No. of crew..21-27.
Named by ....Mrs. Jess Webb, wife of Mr.
....Kenneth Webb, Chairman of
.... Bird's Eye Foods Ltd.

FREEZERS

Freezer landings were not sold in the usual manner by auction on the quayside. The frozen volume landed might be down and the price obtained not revealed, and again the long voyages of this type of vessel distort the figures, making it very difficult to set the vessel's performance over the year in the manner usually done for wet fish trawlers.

There were no official figures published detailing freezer trawlers' performances, but from those available for 1968-69 it does seem the Boston company did very well. In 1969, out of the entire twenty-eight whole freezers, Boston's were top with the *Lady Parkes*, which brought back a record 4,169 tonnes from seven trips and 288 days at sea. The *Boston York*, totalled 2,970 tonnes, while 1974 saw the *Lady Parkes* runner-up to the Boyd Line's *Arctic Freebooter* which won the title in the British Freezer Trawler Challenge Competition.

In the chart opposite it will be seen that the Boston company had three freezer trawlers in the top thirty, at placings No.2, *Lady Parkes*, No.14, *Boston Lincoln*, and No.26, *Sir Fred Parkes*.

FINAL PLACINGS
1974 BRITISH FREEZER TRAWLER
CHALLENGE COMPETITION TOP 30

Vessel	Tons	Points
1. *Arctic Freebooter* (Hull)	3,400.6	51,177
2. *Lady Parkes* (Hull)	2,787.8	42,684
3. *Defiance* (Grimsby)	2,878.4	41,326
4. *Farnella* (Hull)	2,954.4	41,218
5. *Southella* (Hull)	2,658.9	40,225
6. *Cordella* (Hull)	2,704.7	38,982
7. *Pict* (Hull)	2,672.1	38,553
8. *St. Jasper* (Hull)	2,598.6	37,826
9. *Swanella* (Hull)	2,443.1	37,399
10. *Dane* (Hull)	2,581.7	36,811
11. *Northella* (Hull)	2,582.8	35,235
12. *St. Jason* (Hull)	2,265.5	33,792
13. *St. Benedict* (Hull)	2,776.6	32,703
14. *Boston Lincoln* (Hull)	2,170.9	32,665
15. *Goth* (Grimsby)	2,170.9	31,970
16. *Norse* (Hull)	2,168.0	30,875
17. *Seafridge Skua* (Hull)	2,036.3	30,554
18. *Kirkella* (Hull)	2,151.6	29,423
19. *St. Jerome* (Hull)	2,099.2	29,334
20. *Arctic Raider* (Hull)	3,056.8	28,515
21. *Criscilla* (Fleetwood)	1,859.1	28,452
22. *Marbella* (Hull)	1,854.6	27,481
23. *Ross Vanguard* (Grimsby)	1,932.3	27,439
24. *Cassio* (Hull)	2,197.1	27,292
25. *Ross Implacable* (Grimsby)	1,851.0	26,097
26. *Sir Fred Parkes* (Hull)	1,672.8	24,837
27. *Conqueror* (Grimsby)	1,855.9	24,205
28. *Seafridge Petrel* (Hull)	1,623.1	23,787
29. *Arab* (Hull)	1,649.2	23,589
30. *Invincible* (Grimsby)	1,629.7	22,803

The Boston Fleet, in 1969, totalled nine stern trawlers, 59 side trawlers and thirty seine net vessels with two more seine-netters to join their fleet and two medium sized stern trawlers planned.

A SELECTION OF SIDE TRAWLERS OWNED OVER THE YEARS BY BOSTON'S IN HULL.

St. Christopher H573 awaiting the tide to enter St. Andrew's Dock. Photograph courtesy Donald Innes Studio.

Sold to J. Marr & Son in 1951, the St. Crispin H399, seen here in the Humber, was renamed Junella and later became Farnella. Photograph courtesy Donald Innes Studios.

St. Mark H520 was wrecked in 1954. Photograph courtesy Donald Innes Studios.

After three changes of ownership the Prince Philip H32, under her last name of Stella Rigel H170 was wrecked off the north Norway coast in December 1962. All the crew were saved. Photograph courtesy Donald Innes Studios.

The 165ft. trawler St. Christopher H88, transferred to Grimsby in 1961, later sold to South Africa as Oratava in 1971. Photograph courtesy Donald Innes Studio.

Boston Fury H252. One of the larger class of vessels (note the high bridge/wheelhouse) which worked out of Hull and later Grimsby. Photograph courtesy Donald Innes Studio.

Sold to Holland in 1953, the Allan Water H420, returned to Lowestoft as the St. David, in the Colne fleet in 1964 who later converted her for oil rig standby work. Photograph courtesy Donald Innes Studios.

Princess Elizabeth H135, later sold to Hellyer Bros and re-named Roderigo. Photograph courtesy Donald Innes Studios.

On 23rd. January 1955, the *Roderigo* was steaming in close company with the *Lorella* H455, whose radar had become faulty. Most of the other trawlers were sheltering at Ritur Huk, but the *Roderigo* and the *Lorella* were going to the assistance of the trawler *Kingston Garnet*. She had been caught in severe weather conditions disabled with a fouled propeller. The *Kingston Garnet*, however, managed to clear her screw and reach shelter, but the *Lorella* and *Roderigo* were now facing severe gale force winds and freezing weather.

For three days, the two vessels were fighting atrocious weather conditions. Unable to go about and run for shelter, they were obliged merely to dodge into the wind. It was on the 26th. January 1955, off Iceland, ninety miles east of the North Cape and that they were overwhelmed by the continual build up of ice and capsized. From the two ships, forty crew-members lost their lives.

For many years, St. Andrew's Dock had been the centre of activity, a hive of industry, employing thousands, on board trawlers and in the associated ancillary industries ashore. Then in 1975, as always, things began to change.

The British fishing industry was experiencing a series of serious problems, problems which even the largest fishing company found it impossible to overcome. Because of foreign national interests, fishing grounds which had traditionally been fished by British fishermen for hundreds of years had become limited, out of bounds to our vessels. Quotas had also been imposed as a conservation measure and fish generally were becoming more scarce every day.

So it was, the Boston company finding it economically impossible to operate, began to withdraw their old distant water side-trawlers from service, a reluctant decision, forced upon them because the limited grounds and quotas were required for their five freezer trawlers.

At 0400 hours on the 3rd. November 1975 the *Arctic Raider* sailed out of St. Andrew's Dock for the last time, heading for her final trip to the Spitzbergen fishing grounds. She had the dubious honour of being the last trawler to sail from there, leaving behind an empty dock, which, for the first time in ninety-two years was devoid of all trawlers.

Many of the Boston company's trawlers were laid idle awaiting their fate, some were delivered to the scrapyard to meet their undignified and untimely end, others escaped destruction to be sold for oil rig work or to other countries and continued fishing.

By May 1988, the St. Andrew's Dock had taken on a completely different appearance, drained of water exposing the mud and silt. The bulldozers had moved in removing landing jetties and quayside buildings and the large slipways were vanishing, a sad end to a once great and proud industry. In their place now, and on the filled in docks, stands a B&Q d.i.y. store, a Bowling Alley and a fast food chain, although, at the far end of the Dock, one relic of the old fishing years remains. Boston's old offices, now occupied by the Sea Fish Authority, still stand as a proud monument to the past.

Adding to the nostalgia, the Boston company had during its existence, expanded in many ways. In its heyday, the company seemed forever to be establishing themselves in one fishing port or another and even before they arrived in Hull, the company was enjoying success in Grimsby.

Built at Aberdeen in 1950, the Lammermuir H105, was sold to the Faroes in 1956 and scrapped 1976. Photograph courtesy Donald Innes Studios.

Chapter Four

Grimsby

Grimsby, the premier fishing port in the world, was an important base for Boston Deep Sea Fisheries. Besides their dozen or so trawlers based there, they had many other interests in the port, one of which was a major interest in the Great Grimsby Coal Salt & Tanning Company.

They were originally named the Grimsby Barking and Tanning Company, until in February 1873, a consortium of Grimsby fishing vessel owners took over, and a company under the new name was born. They played a vital role in the building up of the port's fishing industry and, as they expanded their interests in the U.K., they also ventured abroad as far apart as Portugal, Iceland and Japan. For years the company was referred to affectionately as Cosalt, but it was not until 1968 when the company officially emerged under that name.

There was a time when Cosalt employed over five hundred girls, who braided nets by hand. In the 1920's and 30's, wagons would take raw materials around the streets, delivering to the girls' homes where most kept a braiding frame. Despite many changes in the fishing industry that side of the business remains today, although modern net making machinery has replaced all hand braiding.

For a number of years a man by the name of Tom Goultor had been buying up shares in Cosalt on behalf of the Boston company, until eventually Boston's became the largest share holder in both the Great Grimsby Coal Salt and Tanning Co. and the Grimsby Fish Meal Co. Sir Fred Parkes and his son Basil became directors of Cosalt. Sir Basil Parkes later sold all shares in that company to the Ross family who had already been buying up shares. Carl Ross became Chairman and his son John Managing Director.

It was very difficult times for the Boston Deep Sea Fishing & Ice Co. in their initial move from Boston, Lincs. to Fleetwood, and then to Grimsby, but the company was led by a man of grit and tenacity whose vocabulary contained not the word failure. For a while they did experience losses on commencement of fishing operations from Grimsby, but not for long. Once firmly established in the port they began to grow, investing heavily in other interests in the area. They bought up hundreds of acres of land which certainly proved an excellent investment over the years.

The years of the 1920's were a period of prosperity for the Boston company and indeed the fishing industry in general. During those years the company built up their fleet to a level never equalled or, for that matter, ever likely to be so. The company also ventured into the realm of buying and selling vessels which proved far more profitable than fishing the vessels themselves. In all the years the company traded, they bought and sold about two hundred vessels selling them to over thirty countries, many investing in trawling for the fist time.

THE BOSTON FLEET IN GRIMSBY

One of the main features of Boston's fleet at Grimsby was an interesting variation in design and size. Of these the first of the post-war newly built vessels to arrive was the 170 ft. *Princess Elizabeth* GY590 which came into service toward the end of 1948. Built for their subsidiary, North Cape Steam Fishing Co. she was later transferred to Hull and renamed *St. Ronan* H86. Sailing from Hull on the 12th. October 1952, outward bound for the fishing grounds, she was wrecked off St. Johns Point, Caithness. There were no casualties.

The next ship did not arrive until 1950 when they took delivery of the *St. Richard* GY134, owned by the company's St. Andrew's Steam Fishing Co., 131ft. long and of 289 gross registered tons. She arrived in August, but remained only one month, making the occasional trip, before her transfer to a subsidiary in Newfoundland. Her fate was sealed when she sank on her first trip out of her new port. Also to arrive in 1950, from the yard of J. Lewis & Co. Ltd of Aberdeen, was GY153 *Boston Fury*. This vessel was the largest to sail from the port until being sold to Faroese owners in 1955.The Beverley yard of Cook, Welton & Gemmell delivered the next post-war distant water trawler for the Great Western Steam Fishing Co. (another subsidiary) in 1956. She was the *Boston Fury* GY188, 577 gross registered tons, with a length of 161ft, followed by her sister ship the *Prince Philip* GY218 which was registered under yet another subsidiary F. &. T. Ross of Hull. Both the *Prince Philip* and the *Boston Fury*, together with another sister ship, the *St. Christopher* H88, were sold to a skipper's co-operative, Abunda Fishing Co. Ltd. to become *Abunda* (*Boston Fury*), *Belgaum* (*Prince Philip*) and *Oratava* (*St. Christopher*). The last mentioned was registered at Grimsby as GY669 and in 1968 she received a new bridge and was renamed *Volesus* before going to Newington Trawlers. Both *Volesus* and *Belgaum* returned to the Boston company under their subsidiaries, the North Cape Fishing Co. and the Iago Steam Fishing Co. in 1974.

Perhaps we all at some time or other compare prices of the old days with those of today and indeed while it is true of modern vessels which today may well exceed grossings of

£100,000 to £300,000, in actual comparison, is there a great deal of difference? Of course living standards have improved and have become more expensive which requires higher wages. The cost of new vessels has accelerated, as have operating costs. Therefore it must follow, returns for our products have to increase in order to pay our way. If we are any better off today it is possibly because we demand higher standards than our parents and grandparents, which again have to be paid for. However, as a matter of interest, the chart below shows actual grossings made by the above vessels for the Skippers Co-operative in 1964 and 1968, the vast difference of which can be seen when compared with landings in 1974.

Both the *Belgaum* and *Volesus* continued fishing for the Boston Company after the Cod Wars with Iceland until, in May 1978, the *Volesus* was sold to Gibraltar, followed in March 1979 by the *Belgaum* which was broken up at Bloor's Wharf, Gravesend. The *Oratava* however had been sold in October 1968 to South African owners and managed to survive the scrapyard until 1983.

Expansion continued during 1956-57 with the arrival of

GRIMSBY DISTANT WATER (All landings are in 10 stone kits)			
10th. April 1964	*Belgaum* (Sk. S. Thorsteinsson) (Norway Coast 24 days)	1,547 kits	£7,471
	Oratava (Sk. J. Nunn) (Norway Coast 22 days)	1,901 kits	£6,728
8th. May 1964	*Oratava* (Sk. J. Nunn) (Iceland 22 days)	1,301 kits	£6,842
	Abunda (Sk. A. Brown) (Iceland 18 days)	1,759 kits	£6,266
12th. Jan 1968	*Oratava* (Sk. D. Sherriff) (Iceland. 22 days)	1,852 kits	£8,657

VOLESUS 1974			
29th Feb 1974	(Iceland 24 days)	594 kits	£10,689
29th March 1974	(Iceland 26 days)	2,450 kits	£32,127
19th April 1974	(Iceland 20 days)	1,335 kits	£17,600
10th May 1974	(Iceland 21 days)	987 kits	£11,629
7th June 1974	(Iceland 22 days)	1,769 kits.	£17,153
28th June 1974	(Iceland 19 days)	2,208 kits	£15,194
19th July 1974	(Iceland 18 days)	2,511 kits	£25,023

VOLESUS 1974 (Continued)			
27th. Sept. 1974	(Iceland 21 days)	1,593 kits	£21,452
25th. Oct. 1974	(Iceland 22 days)	1,487 kits	£22,925
13th. Dec. 1974	(White Sea 23 days)	1,265 kits	£18,037
Totals for that year	10 trips, 216 days	16,209 kits	£191,829

Skippers for that year were: T.B. Evens, A. Hollington, A. Hollingworth and D. Sherriff.

BELGAUM 1974			
11th. Jan. 1974	(Iceland 24 days)	968 kits	£18,336
8th. Feb. 1974	(Iceland 22 days)	1,379 kits	£25,217
8th. March 1974	(Iceland 25 days)	1,526 kits	£25,278
5th. April 1974	(Iceland 22 days)	1,685 kits	£23,742
3rd. May 1974	(Iceland 21 days)	1,842 kits	£18,624
24th. May 1974	(Iceland 22 days)	1,234 kits	£14,670
21st. June 1974	(Iceland 22 days	2,334 kits	£29,203
2nd. Aug. 1974	(Iceland 19 days)	2,392 kits	£34,029
30th. Aug. 1974	(Iceland 22 days)	1,800 kits	£18,954
20th. Sept. 1974	(Iceland 20 days)	1,800 kits	£28,746
11th. Oct. 1974	(Iceland 20 days)	992 kits	£14,046
8th. Nov. 1974	(Iceland 22 days)	1,420 kits	£21,984
29th. Nov. 1974	(White Sea 23 days)	1,116 kits	£19,002
Totals for that year	13 trips, 284 days	20,488 kits	£291,831
Skipper J. Stevens, 6 trips	Skipper T. Whitcombe, 7 trips		

several new vessels for the Boston Deep Sea Fisheries and their subsidiaries. First to arrive in October of that year was the 109 ft. *Boston Valetta*, GY333, built by J. Lewis of Aberdeen, registered to the Don Fishing Co. of Aberdeen, and measuring 239 gross registered tons. That vessel was followed in August 1957 by the arrival from the yard of T. Michison of Newcastle of the *Boston Comet* GY410, 113 ft. in length and gross tonnage of 249. During the same month, the *Boston Vanguard* GY421 entered service. She came from the yard of Vosper Ltd., of Portsmouth; her tonnage was 227 gross and she was 116 ft. long. Both those vessels were registered with the St. Andrew's Steam Fishing Co., Hull. The *Boston Vanguard* was named by Mrs. Snelling and at the launching ceremony the party on the launching platform received a dousing when they were showered with champagne.

After only a brief sojourn in Grimsby, the *Boston Comet* was transferred to the Canadian subsidiary Acadia Fisheries in April 1959. That company renamed her *Rupert Brand IV* and in June 1961, she was followed by the *Boston Valetta* and given a new name *Acadia Finfare*. On her return to Great Britain in 1968, she joined Boston's Lowestoft fleet as LT256 and soon afterwards she reverted to her original name. After working until 1971 she was sold to Pounds of Portsmouth for scrapping. However, instead, she won a reprieve, when, finding a new lease of life, she was acquired by the Dundale Co., of Douglas, Isle of Man, who renamed her *Lady Cora*. Her charmed life continued when she returned to Lowestoft in 1974 for oil rig work, finally being laid up in Earle's yard where she was eventually scrapped in March 1982.

The *Boston Vanguard* was the last of the three trawlers to leave. She was sold in November 1962 into French ownership and became *Imprevu* LR5003, but three years later, the Lowestoft firm of Small & Co. brought her back to England where she was renamed *Suffolk Enterprise* LT492. Colne Fishing Co. took her over in November 1974 renaming her *St. James*. Under their flag she fished for a further six years before being converted for oil rig stand-by work, until on 21st August 1986 when she sailed for the Thames Shipbreakers to be scrapped.

Ordered by the Boston company in 1958, they took delivery of the *Boston Coronet* GY596 in February 1959. Built as a near water trawler by Richards of Lowestoft, her 199 gross registered tonnage was supported by a length of 106 ft. Transferred to Lowestoft in 1962 as LT459 she worked from there until 1980 when, with the fishing industry in a sad decline, she was sold into Spanish interests with the new name *Lidia Prima*.

Three modern diesel trawlers were built for the Boston company at the Beverley shipyard of Cook, Welton & Gemmell in 1958-59. They were 180 ft. in length and all of a gross tonnage of around 691 and 699. Two went to Hull as the *Prince Charles* H77 and *William Wilberforce* H200 where they both earned an excellent reputation as successful vessels. The third was sent to the company's French subsidiary, Pecheries De La Morinie, and registered at Boulogne as the *Saint Louis*. She also became a top trophy winner taking the French fishing industry's coveted Riband Bleu award.

After nine very successful fishing years in France, she was transferred to Grimsby to become *Boston Comanche* GY144. Two months later she was joined by the *William Wilberforce* and both vessels continued their successful reputations from that port. The *Boston Camanche* really smashed the world landings record in January 1974 with a grossing of £60,582 from a twenty-seven days trip to the White Sea grounds. Under the command of Skipper A. Hollington, she landed a catch of 2,752 ten stone kits to exceed the previous record by over £9,000. Unfortunately her new found fame lasted only ninety minutes when it was stolen by Newington Trawlers' modern stern fresher the *C.S. Forester*.

Good fortune for the *Boston Comanche* was to continue throughout the year. Her performance for 1974 was especially creditable, top trawler that year. With an annual grossing of £410,851, she had beaten B.U.T.'s *Ross Revenge* which had been top trawler for 1972/73 by the mere sum of £297. She also came third in the daily earning table with a daily average of £1,407. Three skippers shared command of her for the year, namely, Albert Hollington (one trip), Ray Evans (nine trips) and record breaking Skipper Colin Newton. As with so many other trawlers of that time, the *William Wilberforce* and *Boston Comanche* were victims of a failing industry, speedily heading for redundancy and, condemned for scrap. The *William Wilberforce* was broken up at Drapers , Victoria Dock, Hull in March 1979, followed in October by the *Boston Comanche*. She went to Bloor's Wharf. Rainham in Kent.

The addition of diesel side trawlers to the Grimsby fleet can really only be considered over a period of not more than the ten-and-half years between December 1954 and April 1965, the peak years being 1958/61 when new trawlers were appearing regularly. Their popularity waned from 1962 when trawling companies concentrated their interests on the new modern stern trawler.

Vosper's Portsmouth Ltd. delivered two identical vessels in 1960 to join the Boston company's Grimsby fleet. They became *Parkroyd* GY465 and *Haselbech,* GY628. Both vessels were 113 ft. long and 310 gross tons. The *Haselbech* was transferred to Lowestoft in September 1966, renamed shortly after arrival to

(Continued on Page 95)

Prince Philip GY218, leaving St. Andrew's Dock. In the background can be seen the distinctive offices of the St. Andrew's Fishing Co., the centre of Boston's operations. The name across the top of the building was later changed to 'Boston Deep Sea Fisheries'. Photograph courtesy Mark Stopper.

Straight from the builder's yard, the Princess Elizabeth GY590 not yet registered, seen here in the Humber. Photograph courtesy Donald Innes Studio.

Volsesus GY188. Photograph courtesy Steve Pulfrey.

Boston Valetta GY 333. Photograph courtesy the late G. Osbon.

*Boston Comet GY 410.
Photograph courtesy Peter
Horsley.*

*Boston Coronet GY 596. Photograph
courtesy P.L.R.S. collection.*

Grimsby tugs seen here manoeuvring the William Wilberforce GY140 in Grimsby Fish Dock. Photograph courtesy T.J.M. Wood.

Boston Comanche GY144, pictured here under her original French name Saint Louis B2803. Photograph courtesy Donald Innes Studio.

Parkroyd GY465, Sir Basil Parkes named this vessel after his father's house in Boston, Lincolnshire. The house, incidentally, was Sir Basil's birth place. Photograph courtesy Steve Pulfrey.

Haselbech GY628, undergoing refit on Grimsby Grid. Photograph courtesy Steve Pulfrey.

The Boston Wasp GY 639, was transferred to Lowestoft in 1968. Later she was wrecked on the Honduras coast. Photograph courtesy P.L.R.S. collection.

Seen here leaving the builder's yard, the new Boston Weelsby GY671, steaming down the Humber for her home port of Grimsby. Photograph courtesy Donald Innes Studios.

become *Boston Shackleton* LT714. 1986 saw her sold to Colne Shipping of Lowestoft and after being renamed again she appeared as the *St. Claude*. Four years later she ended her days at the scrapyard of G.T. Services, Barking.

Parkroyd although sailing out of Fleetwood remained under her Grimsby registration, but in 1970, after moving to Aberdeen she sailed from that port as A161. In 1982 she went to join her sister ship when Colne Shipping acquired her. They renamed her *St. Croix* LT251. Ten years later, she too made her final trip to the breakers yard, broken up by Henderson & Morez of Gravesend.

The diesel side trawlers proved to be extremely successful fishing vessels in the early 60's. The *Parkroyd* and *Haselbech* were joined in 1960 by the *Boston Wasp* GY639, just two feet longer and ten tons less tonnage. She too was transferred to Lowestoft in September 1968 and registered as LT238, under her original name. Later she was sold to the Honduras company of John Borden of Roaton. That vessel was wrecked at La Ceiba on the Honduras coast in 1989.

One of three vessels which joined the Boston fleet in 1961 was the *Boston Weelsby* GY671, from the yard of Cook, Welton & Gemmell of Beverley. With a gross tonnage of 412 and a length of 137 ft., she was built with accommodation for twenty crewmen situated amidships and aft. Her fishroom, lined with timber and insulated with fibreglass, had a capacity of 10,500 cu. ft.

While at sea on a trip in 1968, the *Boston Weelsby* encountered a severe storm, a great sea easily forty feet high rolled upon her, tons of water engulfing her. She rolled violently to a dangerous 70° testing her stability to the limits. Skipper Sid Croft later said, he had never experienced anything like it, he and his crew had hung on to the edge of eternity.

On outward appearance, the *Boston Weelsby* looked little worse for the experience, only the wheelhouse windows required replacement and some damage to the lifeboat aft, but below decks was a different matter. Winch machinery was out of action and serious repairs needed to be made to the electrics. The *Boston Weelsby* was fortunate, in as much as there were no casualties. No-one was lost or injured, and as she returned to port there were no anxious wives or mothers waiting and hoping at the lock-pits, not this time.

On the 17th. July 1969, Mr. Fred Parkes announced that two trawlers were to be sold to South African interests as part of a new deal signed with Irvin & Johnson of Capetown. The two vessels were to be the *Boston Weelsby* and the *Princess Elizabeth*. The same year, both vessels left England for their long voyage South to their new home in warmer climates.

Prior to the departure of both vessels, a new exchange arrival was planned for Grimsby. With a gross tonnage of 442 tons, the 139 ft. *Prince Philip*, built by Hall Russell of Aberdeen, was delivered to Fleetwood in 1963 and registered as FD400. In September 1968 she was exchanged for the newly acquired *Aberdeen Explorer* A765 which was then renamed *Boston Explorer* FD15, and the *Prince Philip* was transferred to Grimsby and became GY138.

Her most outstanding achievement came in 1969. The previous year had already seen her top earner for the port's middle water vessels, with a grossing of £124,871, but not only did the trawler repeat her success, she actually increased her grossing to £170,346 from 30,339 ten stone kits, distinguishing herself as overall top earner over all wet fish trawlers operating out of Grimsby. To achieve this, though, she had made nineteen trips, fourteen of which were under the command of Skipper Walter Nutten, and spent 333 days at sea.

Aberdeen born Skipper Nutten sailed out of his home port from 1935 until 1939 when he was required for war service. He served with the Royal Navy until the end of hostilities and then came to Grimsby, sailing first for B.U.T. and then Northern Trawlers before joining the Boston company in 1966.

The *Prince Philip* had to wait a while before joining the top bracket again. It was not until five years later, in 1974, when under Skipper Albert Hollington, with a grossing of £266,825, she took second place to the *Boston Phantom* (Skipper W. Nutten) which grossed £292,970.

With the loss of the Icelandic grounds and restricted quotas off the Noway Coast, she became another victim of the fishing industry's decline. Converted for oil rig support work she went on charter to Colne Shipping who later purchased her and changed her port of registry to Lowestoft and renamed her *Colne Hunter*. She was scrapped on the 29th. July 1991.

SKIPPER ROY EVANS

Roy Evans came from a well known Grimsby fishing family. His father, Skipper Tom Evans was skipper of the *Boston Concord*, and both his grandfathers were also skippers. Not surprising then that Roy became the youngest skipper to take command of the *Prince Philip*. As a young schoolboy, Roy's father took him on several trips to sea, which, according to his mother, strongly influenced his decision to make a career in the industry.

After leaving school he attended the Boulevard Nautical College in Hull until at fifteen years of age he made his first serious trip as a deckie learner. He was only nineteen when he qualified simultaneously as third hand and mate, and he immediately obtained an appointment as second hand, making one North sea trip while awaiting the return of his father. Thereafter, taking his books with him to study when opportunity offered, he sailed as mate in the *Boston Concord*. By the age of twenty-one, Roy had sat for and gained his skipper's ticket, and the Boston company lost no time in giving him his first command, the *Prince Philip*. Below is his record of landings for the year 1974. Only the first two were made in the *Prince Philip*, the remaining nine in the *Boston Comanche*.

28th Feb	26 days	Iceland	1,500 kits	£18,101
22nd March	20 days	Iceland	1,249 kits	£21,626
26th April	22 days	Iceland	1,621 kits	£19,969
24th May	24 days	Bear Island	2,351 kits	£30,271
14th June	21 days	Iceland	2,134 kits	£26,332
26th July	21 days	Iceland	2,476 kits	£27,072
16th Aug	21 days	Iceland	2,656 kits	£31,759
4th Oct	22 days	Iceland	1,722 kits	£22,752
25th Oct	21 days	Iceland	1,647 kits	£25,311
22nd Nov	22 days	White Sea	2,294 kits	£24,079
27th Dec	24 days	Bear Island	2,389 kits	£31,018

Grimsby will remember the *Boston Concord* GY730 as the last side trawler to be built for the Boston company in that port. She was delivered in April 1965 having been constructed in the Polish shipyard at Gdynia.

Among those attending the naming ceremony were the British Consul of Gdynia, Mr. J. A. Forward, Ship surveyor of Lloyds register Mr. M. Pycinski and his wife, and from Boston Deep Sea Fisheries, Mr. Fred Parkes and Mr. Harriss. The naming ceremony was actually performed by Mrs. Halma Niemyt.

Measuring 758 gross registered tons and 185 ft long, the vessel was of sturdy design. Although transferred to the Boston owned St Andrew's Steam Fishing Co. she remained in Grimsby.

She made many good trips in her comparatively short working life, before she too became a premature victim. She sailed to the breakers yard in Dartford, Kent in December 1980.

BOSTON LINCOLN GY1399

Just before 9pm on Easter Saturday 1968 there arrived in Grimsby on the evening tide, a large new wet fish stern trawler. Her name was *Boston Lincoln* GY1399. All of 212 ft. in length, she was largest trawler in the wet fish fleet, from the Polish shipyard of Stocznia Im Komuny Paraskiej of Gdynia.

With just a skeleton crew and senior executive of the Boston company as passengers, her skipper, W. Balls safely delivered her.

Investing in such a large wet fish vessel, the company had noted the success of similar vessels in France which were currently making top grossings in the port of Boulogne. How to utilise the high catching potential of the vessel would create problems for her skipper, considering the relatively short time a distant water trawler has on the fishing grounds.

The company closely monitored the ship's performance with a view to discovering if her size and speed would enable her to put enough fish in her spacious fish room to improve upon her smaller counterparts of the distant water fleet.

On her maiden fishing trip to the Icelandic grounds, Skipper Balls experienced considerable difficulty with the vessel's trim. Because of that, her fishing time was reduced to only five days. On her return she landed 1,713 kits to gross £8,448.

It was decided in the following year 1969 to convert the *Boston Lincoln* into a freezer. In October she entered the William Wright Dry Dock to be stretched adding a further 27 ft. 7ins. to her length. After the Humber St. Andrews Engineering Co. had completed the task, refrigeration and cold store plant were installed.The alterations and refit were completed in March 1970 at a total cost of £150,000.

As a matter of interest, it may be worthy of note that during the nine months spent as a Fresher she had made fourteen trips, landing 37,163 kits to realise £152,373. Imagine!, had she spent the full year in that role she could have exceeded the £200,0000 barrier. In July 1971 she was transferred from Grimsby to Hull, joining the company's other three freezers, thus allowing the freezer operation to be concentrated in the one port.

Trawler agents, I.F.O.S. Ltd. chartered the *Boston Lincoln* for a six months exploratory trip to the Patagonia fishing grounds off Argentina. She also undertook trials in the Falklands in September 1972, but her discoveries of lucrative fishing grounds around the Falklands led to the present day intensive exploits of those grounds. Painted white she sailed south under the command of Skipper George Downs.

During her stay there, the *Boston Lincoln* spent half her time in port undertaking repairs. Even then, she found immense shoals of hake, so dense, she could have taken 200/300 tonnes a day. When this news reached the government of Argentina they immediately declared a 100 mile fishing limit, a typical ploy, after others had done the groundwork at great expense.

In March 1973, Skipper Stan Taylor had taken over

Prince Philip FD400, pictured here when registered at Fleetwood before her transfer to Grimsby to become GY138. Photograph courtesy Maritime Photo Library.

Boston Concord GY730. Photograph courtesy Steve Pulfrey.

Built in the same Polish shipyard as the Boston Concord, Boston Boeing GY183, was originally owned by Boston's associate French company Pecheries De La Morinie as the St. Luc. She was transfered to Grimsby in 1970 where she remained until 1980 when she was scrapped. Photograph courtesy Donald Innes Studios.

Boston Lincoln GY1399. Photograph courtesy Steve Pulfrey.

command, and the vessel returned to England. The company decided any future fishing on those grounds would require a large factory ship with bigger crew. Therefore the *Boston Lincoln* returned to her old haunts on the Arctic grounds, until, after the troubled times of the Cod Wars with Iceland she was laid up in Hull docks.

Some time later she was transferred to Lowestoft under the management of Boston Putford, who assigned her to work as a Trinity House Guard Vessel. The last of the Boston company's large freezer trawlers, she was sold in 1985 to Panama converted for standby work under a new name *Maria De Lurdes Viepra* where she still remains.

SPECIFICATIONS OF *BOSTON LINCOLN*

Port of Reg. and Number . . . . .GY 1399
Official No 333948
Tonnage . . . . .Gross Reg..846
Net. 285
Length . . . . .212 ft.
Beam . . . . .39.4 ft.
Builder .Stocznia Im Komuny
Paraskiej of Gdynia
Year Built 1968
Lengthened in 1970 to. . . . . .237.7 ft.
Increasing her tonnage to . . . . .994 gross
(374 net)
Type . . . . .Fresher converted to Freezer

Factory details:
Fish Hold . . . . .21,200 cu. ft.
Later to . . . . .30,000 cu. ft.
Freezers .5 Jackstone Froster
V.P.Freezers capable of freezing
45 tons per day
Sept 1972 . . . . .2 Baader 433 Headers installed

Engine details
. . . . .Mirrlees National Ltd. Type KLSSMR 8.
. . . . .2,600 B.H.P.
. . . . .Speed 15.5 knots.

Launched . . . . .30th. Sept. 1967
Skipper (Maiden voyage) . . . . .W.G. Balls
No. of crew . . . . .22-28.
Named by . . . . .Mrs. E. Tee, wife of Lloyds'
Representative in Poland

SKIPPER W.G. BALLS

At the age of fifteen years, Skipper Balls began his career in the fishing industry with Consolidated Fisheries Ltd. He gained his certificate of competence as Skipper six years later, after which he successively commanded the trawlers, *Norwich City*, *Hull City*, *Arsenal* and *Everton*, before moving over to Bostons', who appointed him skipper of the *Abunda* (*Volesus*), followed by the *William Wilberforce* to become one of the Boston company's top skippers.

Paying a price believed to be in the region of £$1/2$m., the Boston Deep Sea Fisheries took delivery of the 121 ft. *Boston Halifax* in 1975. Skipper Tom Smith, a distant water skipper, took her on her maiden voyage which had to be the offshore banks, outside the newly imposed fifty mile Icelandic limit. Later, with the British fleet banned from Icelandic waters, the company was forced to switch her to work the Norwegian coast from where she returned in November 1978 to land 1,423 kits grossing £45,868, top vessel for that week.

In extremely contrasting fortunes, an atmosphere of unrelieved gloom set the pattern for 1978. The European Economic Community had again failed to obtain any worthwhile agreements with third countries. Brussels had succeeded in decimating even the remnants of what remained of a once mighty distant water fishing fleet.

It was a depressing sight as the year ended to see all the port's large deep sea trawlers laid up without making one single trip in that year. Only seventy-one distant water trips were made in 1978, and those by a mere handful of freshers mostly in the first six months.

As winter approached we find the *Boston Halifax* was the port's only solitary distant water vessel still working the north east Arctic grounds and she landed the last trip by a Grimsby distant water trawler on 14th. December. After twenty-four days she returned from the Norway coast, under Skipper Ray Harris to put ashore only 778 kits which made a mere £28,018.

Only a few days after making that meagre landing, the *Boston Halifax*, last of the Boston company's fleet to land in the port, slipped quietly out of port almost un-noticed, on its way to join the company's expanding Lowestoft fleet. She was later re-registered LO339 in 1985, and 1986 saw her sold to Denmark.

Tighter fishing restrictions contributed to crippling losses, which in turn created a withdrawal of the Boston Deep Sea Fisheries' Grimsby vessels from the seas.

So it was, in September of the same year, the fishing community of Grimsby were shocked when it was announced by

Mr. Fred Parkes jnr. that, after fifty years in Grimsby, the company were leaving. It was indeed the end of an era. The company had not taken the decision lightly, in fact it was with the utmost reluctance, but traditional distant water fishing was considerably reduced for this Country.

A massive sale of property in Grimsby followed the withdrawl which was handled by the Fred Parkes Holding Co.

Although Boston Deep Sea Fisheries had departed, the company of Fred Parkes Holdings remained. In fact in September 1979 they bought the 196 ft. *Najala* from Norway. She had been built at Harstad in 1978 and on arrival in Grimsby she was renamed *Grimsby Lady* GY430. Powered by a MAK 3,400 h.p. engine, she carried the extraordinary beam of 36 ft. and entering Grimsby dock for the first time she barely managed to squeeze through the lock pit.

Operated by the Sandee Fishing Co. Ltd., which was part of the Fred Parkes Holdings, the vessel's size demanded an annual grossing of £800,000 to make her viable.

The *Grimsby Lady* was designated to first sail for the Scottish west coast grounds for mackerel, then at the end of the season to fish for blue whiting.

Under the command of Skipper Andy Jenson she also carried on board a Faroese fishing advisor and some Faroese crew, but her stay in Grimsby was comparatively short. Sold back to Norway, she became *Ydal*.

The same company also owned three smaller inshore fishing vessels, which were under another off-shoot of the Holding Company and were operated by the Tom Sleight Ltd. agency, again a part of the same parent company.

Built at the Renfrew yard of Argyll Ship & Boatbuilding Co. the *Mohave* GY309, a seventy-four feet multi-purpose trawler, was propelled by a Mirrlees Blackstone ERSL 6 MR four stroke cycle diesel. Former distant water Skipper Derek Brown took her on her maiden voyage. Leaving the Renfrew yard, she was forced to put in to Oban for minor repairs before proceeding to Stornoway to take on ice.

The second of this new type of vessel was the *Shawnee* GY310, (Skipper Ray Harris another top distant water skipper). She later paired up with the *Mohave*.

Finally the third arrival of that class, the *Sioux* GY311 was skippered by Portuguese born John Oliveira-Lota, a native of Setubal. He worked her out of North Shields although she was based at Grimsby.

Both the *Mohave* and the *Shawnee* made record breaking landings in Grimsby, their revolutionary design proving advantageous.

The restraints which had evolved in the British fishing industry were, to say the least, most frustrating. Restrictive practices imposed on us were very discouraging, but added to those, 1977 turned out to be a disastrous year for all of the three small vessels.

In early January with thirty tonnes of mackerel stowed on one side of her fish room, the *Shawnee* was swamped by the incoming tide. The crew, although sleeping at the time, escaped safely. She was towed to Falmouth for further damage reports.

A very tragic event happened in March of that year, when after catching fire the *Sioux* went down in gale force winds and blinding snow showers. She was about thirty-six miles east of the Humber. Her Skipper Norman Howe, in true, archetypal seafaring tradition, made certain his small crew of five were safely in the life raft before he himself jumped for the raft. He, sadly was swept away and lost. Later, after a morning's search by the Humber Lifeboat, *City of Bradford*, on its first ever call out, his body was recovered, still in his life jacket, from the sea.

Mohave and *Shawnee*, were instantly laid up as a precautionary measure until the results of the *Sioux's* foundering were promulgated. Later, both vessels were sold, to Delga Shipping, a subsidiary of Colne Shipping and transferred to Lowestoft. Eventually they were both sold to France.

MANAGERS AT GRIMSBY

During the fifty years the Boston company were operating out of Grimsby, only three men have held the envious position of trawler manager. The post demanded a special kind of man, a man capable of handling fishermen. More often than not they were rough diamonds, tough and as hardy as any fisherman, who commanded the respect of all who worked under them. The manager's job, among his many duties, entailed the day to day running of the trawlers, ordering fuel, supplies and organising ships' rosters besides acting as wages clerk. When things went a little wrong, it was the manager, probably with the skipper who was on the carpet.

The three men who aspired to the post of manager at Grimsby were, Charles Wrack, Burt Warman and Murdoc Macinnes. Charles Wrack joined the Boston Deep Sea Fishing Co. in its early days while based in their initial port of Boston, Lincolnshire, and remained in their employment for fifty years.

An accomplished sportsman, Charlie, for many years combined work on the Fish Docks with a very successful first and second division league soccer career, playing both for Grimsby Town and Hull City. Playing centre half, he captained

Built at Goole in 1975, the Boston Halifax GY321, pictured here on trials in the Humber. Photograph courtesy Walter Fussey & Son.

Arriving in Grimsby in 1972, the Boston Beverley GY191 is referred to in more detail in the Chapter on Fleetwood. Photograph courtesy Steve Pulfrey.

the Mariners when Grimsby won promotion from the second to first division in 1929.

Charlie officially retired in 1967 and the Boston company took the unusual step of presenting him with a retirement gift of the fish merchanting business, F. & B. A. Parkes, a nice gesture after fifty years loyal service. He continued as a full time merchant for a few years and at the age of seventy-nine, he passed away.

The following list gives us some idea of the numerous vessels which passed through the Boston company's hands during their long stay in Grimsby.

And so another chapter in the history of the Boston Deep Sea Fisheries ended. It seems all that remains are nostalgic recollections of a once great fishing fleet, manned by expert fishermen. But it was not sentiment which motivated the Boston company. Its successful growth and prosperity were achieved by sheer business acumen. Having established themselves in Fleetwood, Hull, Grimsby and abroad, they knew Lowestoft was ripe for them.

DETAILS OF TRAWLERS BOUGHT AND SOLD BY BOSTON D.S.F.
MANY OF THESE WERE ACQUIRED AND DISPOSED OF
BETWEEN THE TWO WORLD WARS

VESSEL	Reg. No.	Where Built	Gr. Ton.	Length	Notes
Yulan	GY 348	London 1891	144	96ft.	Bought Oct. 1935-sold July 1945 to Wendover Fishing Co.
Wisteria	GY 302	London 1891	143	96ft.	Bought Oct. 1935-sold Oct. 1935 to Consol F.
Chanticleer	GY 124	Beverley 1894	173	114ft.	Bought Sept. 1925-sold Dec. 1947 to France, became Heniville.
Draco	GY 842	Govan 1895	139	99ft.	Bought Feb. 1922 from Newhaven.
Sea Hawk	GY1251	Aberdeen 1898	169	108ft.	Bought 1925-sold April 1928 to Plymouth.
St. Cloud	GY 856	Hull 1899	193	108ft.	Bought Sept.1925-scrapped 1928.
King Eric	GY 984	Selby 1899	260	125ft.	Bought May 1940 from T.W. Baskcomb. Torpedoed by U141 off Iceland 6th. Sept. 1941.

DETAILS OF TRAWLERS BOUGHT AND SOLD BY BOSTON D.S.F. (Continued)
MANY OF THESE WERE ACQUIRED AND DISPOSED OF BETWEEN THE TWO WORLD WARS

VESSEL	Reg. No.	Where Built	Gr. Ton.	Length	Notes
Quassia	GY1141	Grimsby 1900	207	116ft.	Bought Oct. 1933-sold Nov. 1935 to C. Dobson.
Ranee	GY1157	Hull 1900	194	110ft.	Bought June 1941-sold Oct. 1943 to Gt. Gy. & E. Coast S.F. Co.
Robinia	GY1147	Grimsby 1900	208	116ft.	Bought Oct. 1935-sold Nov. 1935 to F. Moss.
Weymouth	GY 386	North Shields 1903	178	110ft.	Bought Oct. 1935-scrapped March 1936.
Glenroy	GY 817	Dundee 1905	137	100ft.	Bought Sept. 1925-sold August 1928.
Romilly	GY 437	Selby 1905	214	117ft	Bought Nov. 1952-scrapped 1955.
Lord Rothschild	GY 718	Govan 1906	174	112ft.	Bought Dec. 1917-sold Aug. 1918 to W.W. Butt.
Octavia	GY 102	Beverley 1906	173	108ft.	Bought Oct. 1925-sold Jan. 1926 to Hull.
Soranus	GY 225	Selby 1906	250	127ft.	Bought Nov. 1939-sold Oct. 1942 to Northern Trawlers.
Triton	GY 384	Dundee 1907	230	120ft.	Bought Oct. 1935-sold Oct. 1935 to C. Dobson.
Marlborough	GY 306	Selby 1907	213	115ft.	Bought Nov. 1952 TWLRS GY Ltd. Scrapped Jan. 1955.
Great Admiral	GY 733	Beverley 1908	284	135ft.	Bought Oct. 1935-scrapped Nov. 1947.
Magnolia	GY 482	Beverley 1909	260	125ft.	Bought Oct. 1935-sold Oct. 1935 to H. Franklin.

DETAILS OF TRAWLERS BOUGHT AND SOLD BY BOSTON D.S.F. (Continued)
MANY OF THESE WERE ACQUIRED AND DISPOSED OF
BETWEEN THE TWO WORLD WARS

VESSEL	Reg. No.	Where Built	Gr. Ton.	Length	Notes
Minoru	GY 484	Beverley 1909	260	125ft.	Bought Oct. 1935-sold Oct. 1935 to Dobson ship RPG Co.
Xylopia	GY1306	Selby 1911	262	125ft.	Bought Oct 1935-sold Oct. 1935 to C. Dobson.
Escallonia	GY 631	Beverley 1911	285	132ft.	Bought Oct. 1935-scrapped 1938.
Hondo	GY 701	Selby 1912	229	135ft.	Bought Sept. 1935-scrapped Nov. 1947.
Rowsley	GY 751	Beverley 1912	213	117ft.	Bought June 1941-sold Oct. 1941 to Aberdeen.
Raetia	GY 707	Beverley 1912	261	130ft.	Bought Jan 1942-scrapped 1946.
The Tetrarch	GY 947	Beverley 1913	223	117ft.	Bought Oct. 1935-sold Oct. 1935 to Dobson Ship RPG Co.
Scarron	GY 935	Beverley 1913	296	130ft.	Bought Jan. 1942-Scrapped Nov. 1946.
Sweeper	GY 853	Beverley 1913	395	150ft.	Bought Sept. 1935-sold Mar. 1936 to Norway. Sunk by U714 1945.
Unita	GY 924	Beverley 1913	296	130ft.	Bought Jan. 1942-sold Mar. 1946 to Nordic S.F.
Barle	GY 78	Selby 1914	283	135ft.	Bought Oct. 1935-lost 1st. April 1936, West Coast, Scotland.
War Wing	GY 837	Beverley 1915	226	117ft.	Bought Oct. 1935-sold Oct. 1935.
Winooka	GY 463	Beverley 1915	331	137ft.	Bought Oct. 1935-sunk after collision in North Sea, 15/3/36.
Sea King	GY1251	Selby 1916	321	138ft.	Bought March 1934-sunk off Grimsby Sept. 1940.

DETAILS OF TRAWLERS BOUGHT AND SOLD BY BOSTON D.S.F. (Continued)
MANY OF THESE WERE ACQUIRED AND DISPOSED OF
BETWEEN THE TWO WORLD WARS

VESSEL	Reg. No.	Where Built	Gr. Ton.	Length	Notes
Seddon	GY 991	Beverley 1916	296	130ft.	Bought Jan 1942-sold April 1946 to London owners.
Sethon	GY 928	Beverley 1916	295	130ft.	Bought Jan. 1942-sold 1946.
Sarpedon	GY 984	Beverley 1916	344	135ft.	Bought Jan. 1942-sold 1947 to Anglo S.F.
Fontenay	GY 397	Canada 1917	271	125ft.	Bought Sept. 1926-sold Oct. 1926 to France. Became *Marie Roselyne*.
Marie Evelyne	GY 398	Canada 1917	272	125ft.	Bought Sept. 1926-sold Oct. 1926 to France.
Malaga	GY 474	Canada 1917	271	125ft.	Bought Sept. 1926-missing since 18th. Oct. 1935.
Moravia	GY1018	Beverley 1917	306	130ft.	Bought Jan. 1942 sunk by mine North Sea, (R.N. Service) 1943.
Ogano	GY 69	Beverley 1917	265	125ft.	Bought June 1945-sold Feb. 1945 to Ogano S.F.
Olympia	GY1080	Beverley 1917	261	120ft.	Bought Jan. 1942-sold Jan. 1946 to Milford Haven.
Kastoria	GY1017	Beverley 1917	307	130ft.	Bought Jan. 1942-sold April 1947 to Poland.
Ceylonite	GY 170	Beverley 1918	249	125ft.	Bought June 1939-sold Dec. 1947.
Somersby (1)	GY 390	Canada 1918	271	125ft.	Bought Sept. 1926-sold May 1937 to London owners.
William Hanbury	GY1225	Leith 1918	204	115ft.	Bought Feb. 1940-Ran aground May 1942, lost.

DETAILS OF TRAWLERS BOUGHT AND SOLD BY BOSTON D.S.F. (Continued)
MANY OF THESE WERE ACQUIRED AND DISPOSED OF
BETWEEN THE TWO WORLD WARS

VESSEL	Reg. No.	Where Built	Gr. Ton.	Length	Notes
Hagnaby	GY 203	Troon 1918	277	125ft.	Bought Feb. 1925-sold May 1927 to Spain.
Willoughby	GY 161	Paisley 1918	329	138ft.	Bought Feb. 1925-sold Feb. 1928 to Iceland.
Clixby	GY 180	Greenock 1918	281	125ft.	Bought Feb. 1925-sold July 1926 to France. Became *Antimone II*.
Evelyn Rose	GY 9	Selby 1918	327	138ft.	Bought May 1936-sold Aug. 1945 to Fleetwood, lost 1954.
St. Minver	GY 438	Goole 1919	323	138ft.	Bought May 1936-sold to Admiralty Jan. 1940.
Keelby	GY 205	Lowestoft 1919	274	123ft.	Bought Feb. 1925-sold July 1926 to France. Became *La Banche II*.
Somersby (2)	GY 208	Lowestoft 1919	274	125ft.	Bought Feb. 1925-sold Aug. 1926 to France. Became *Les Barges*.
Daily Telegraph	GY 367	Selby 1920	328	140ft.	Bought May 1931-sold Sept. 1933, to France. Became *La Vierge*,
Margaret Rose	GY 355	Selby 1931	409	144ft.	Bought March 1931-sold to France Aug. 1933, became *Marguerete Rose*.
Leeds United	GY 261	Middlesboro' 1933	339	135ft.	Bought June 1963-sold Sept. 1963.
Princess Elizabeth (1)	GY 590	Beverley 1948	568	170ft.	Dealt with elsewhere.
Boston Fury (1) (Brandur 1966)	GY 153 GY 111	Aberdeen 1950	760	185ft.	Sold to Faroes 1955-rebought Mar. 1966- sold July 1966 to Weelsby Trawlers Ltd. Scrapped 1968.

DETAILS OF TRAWLERS BOUGHT AND SOLD BY BOSTON D.S.F. (Continued)
MANY OF THESE WERE ACQUIRED AND DISPOSED OF
BETWEEN THE TWO WORLD WARS

VESSEL	Reg. No.	Where Built	Gr. Ton.	Length	Notes
St. Richard	GY 134	Hessle 1950	289	131ft.	Dealt with elsewhere.
North Cape	GY 75	Beverley 1951	574	170ft.	Bought Sept. 1959-from Belgium, ex. Van Oust.
North Holme	GY 76	Beverley 1951	576	166ft.	Bought Sept. 1959-from Belgium, ex. Van Eyck.
Prince Philip (Belgaum 1961)	GY 218	Beverley 1956	577	160ft.	Dealt with elsewhere.
St. Bartholomew	GY 178	Beverley 1953	635	175ft.	Sold to Belgium 1954.
Boston Valet	GY 333	Aderdeen 1956	239	109ft.	Dealt with elsewhere.
Boston Fury (2) (Abunda) (Volesus)	GY 188	Beverley 1956	577	160ft.	Sold to North Cape Fisheries Feb. 1974. Scrapped 1978.
Boston Vanguard	GY 421	Portsmouth 1957	243	112ft.	Sold 1962 to France. Became Imprevu, later to Lowestoft as St. James.
Boston Comet	GY 410	Newcastle 1957	249	113ft.	Dealt with elsewhere.
St. Christopher	GY 669	Beverley 1958	603	160ft.	Renamed Oratava, sold to South Oct. 1968.
Boston Coronet	GY 596	Lowestoft 1959	199	105ft.	Sold 1980 to Spain. Became Lidia Prima .
William Wilberforce	GY 140	Beverley 1959	698	179ft	Trans' Oct. 1974-scrapped 1978.

DETAILS OF TRAWLERS BOUGHT AND SOLD BY BOSTON D.S.F. (Continued)
MANY OF THESE WERE ACQUIRED AND DISPOSED OF
BETWEEN THE TWO WORLD WARS

VESSEL	Reg. No.	Where Built	Gr. Ton.	Length	Notes
Boston Comanche	GY 144	Beverley 1959	616	179ft.	Ex *St. Louis*. Bought Nov. 1968. Scrapped 1979.
Haselbech	GY 628	Portsmouth 1960	310	112ft.	Transferred to Lowestoft 1968 became *Boston Shackleton*.
Boston Wasp	GY 639	Aberdeen 1960	300	114ft.	Transferred to Lowestoft Sept. 1968.
Boston Tristar	GY 210	Aberdeen 1960	434	139ft.	July 1972 transferred to-sold to Colne Shipping 1976.
Boston Weelsby	GY 671	Beverley 1961	412	137ft.	Sold to South Africa 1969.
Boston Concord	GY 730	Poland 1965	758	185ft.	Scrapped Oct. 1980.
Boston Lincoln	GY1399	Poland 1968	846	195ft.	Stretched by 25ft. in 1984, increased to 944g.r.t. and 220ft.
Princess Elizabeth	GY 143	Beverley 1961	419	139ft.	Sold to South Africa 1969.
Boston Boeing	GY 183	Poland 1962	707	196ft.	Bought Sept. 1970, ex *St. Luc*. Scrapped 1980.
Prince Philip	GY 138	Aberdeen 1963	442	140ft.	Dealt with elsewhere.
Boston Beverley	GY 191	Hessle 1971	517	140ft.	Sold 1980 to Chile.
Boston Halifax	GY 321	Goole 1975	387	128ft.	Sold to North Cape Fisheries in 1974.

Chapter Five

Lowestoft

It was during the 1939-45 War when the Boston company purchased quite a number of steam drifter trawlers from various local owners. One fleet purchased was eight in number, all named after 'Lords': *Lord Hood*, *Lord Byron*, *Lord Collingwood* etc., which were sold to them by Mr. Harald Jackson (Colonel) whose brother, incidentally, was Dr. Tom Jackson a solicitor for the Boston company in Hull.

Having acquired this large fleet in East Anglia the company was now faced with a situation where they had no-one to manage their Lowestoft and Yarmouth operations. This was soon overcome by appointing the able Major. A.W. (Bill) Suddaby M.B.E.

As Boston vessels became de-requisitioned by the Admiralty in 1945/46, Boston Deep Sea Fisheries set up an office under Major Suddaby which enabled the company's vessels to land in that port. The first ship to land taking advantage of this, was the North Shore Fishing Company's *Spes Aurea* LT72. This company was a another subsidiary of the parent firm. Under the command of Skipper W. Sandford she landed on the 3rd. January 1946 and for the second time in Lowestoft on 10th. January. The *Spes Aurea* was joined by the *Lord Keith* LT181. She was, registered under the St. Andrew's Steam Fishing Co. of Hull and her skipper was Jack Reeder. On 12th. February 1946 another St. Andrew's vessel landed, the *Lord Suffolk* LT44, followed in March by the *Lord Anson* LT344 (Skipper J. Oakes). She also was the first Boston vessel to land in Yarmouth. Yarmouth was primarily a herring port, and as such white fish were only a secondary commodity. After a few years, trawling operations had almost ceased to exist from there. The Boston company was forced to concentrate their efforts on Lowestoft.

No matter where the Boston Deep Sea Fisheries established themselves, they never relaxed their efforts in improving the position or their image, and so it was, in 1955 the company left their offices in Battery Green Road, to take up new premises in the Columbus Building on the corner of Waveney Road, just opposite the entrance to the fish docks.

For some reason during the company's advent into the port, they experienced difficulties in their relations with some of the port's other operators, even to the extent that some Boston drifters were refused permission to land there, and were forced to land in Yarmouth. However, Bill Suddaby managed to overcome those difficulties and within a few years he had effectively established a good working relationship, with all owners working together. Probably because of his diplomacy and his ability to cement those good relationships, the Major was made president of the British Trawler Federation, the first and only Lowestoft owner to hold the office, and again later in 1969/70 when Managing Director in Hull.

Under his guidance, the Boston company was, for many years, the largest and most important owner in Lowestoft. He had done a first rate job by his contribution towards selling off the old drifter trawlers and replacing them with new modern diesel vessels. After Sir Fred Parkes' death, Basil Parkes invited Major Suddaby to move and become managing director of the Boston Group at the head office in Hull.

The vacancy created by the departure of Bill Suddaby was filled by Peter Catchpole, becoming Boston's manager at Lowestoft at the age of twenty-six. His grandfather, the late Mr. George Catchpole, entered the industry as a fisherman who later went on to own one of the port's biggest drifter fleets. On his retirement George was succeeded by his son Fred, who spent his whole life in the fishing world in Lowestoft.

Peter served for three years as trainee with Associated Fisheries of Grimsby and Hull, which included periods with Northern Trawlers of Grimsby and with the Lord Line, working under Mr. Tom Boyd. He was with the Boston company for a considerable number of years.

After a while he formed his own company, Warbler Shipping Ltd. Later he joined Mr. Fred Parkes Jnr. as Managing Director of the Tom Sleight Group in Grimsby, for whom he managed forty seine net vessels. After three years with them he returned to Lowestoft. Peter is now Managing Director of Boston Putford Offshore Safety Ltd., where he still employs several ex-Boston fishing skippers on oil rig standby work.

Last of the managers for the Boston Deep Sea Fisheries in Lowestoft was Mr. Raymond Prior, who, before burying the anchor, had for quite a while been one of the company's leading skippers. In the thirty-eight years since Bostons' opened an office in Lowestoft, only four men have held that post. Another outstanding manager was, Vernon Green. Vernon had been manager for Bostons in North Shields and he followed Arthur Lewis in Fleetwood, before going on to manage Grimsby, Hull and Lowestoft.

Boston Deep Sea Fisheries built up a significant fleet in Lowestoft. Many of the vessels the company acquired were there temporarily before being sold or moved to other ports or into the

Lord Suffolk LT 44. The Boston Company bought her while on war service in 1943 and sold her to Milford Haven in 1946. She was sold to breakers in 1976. Photograph courtesy Mark Stopper collection.

Lord Keith LT 181. Built in 1930 she also saw war service between 1939-45, bought for St. Andrew's Steam Fishing Co. by the parent firm in 1943. Sold to Cypress owners in 1975. She was reported as being converted to a refrigerated stern trawler. Photograph courtesy P.L.R.S. collection.

Kirkley LT 225. One of the M.F.V. class of vessels built for the Admiralty during the war as M.F.V. 1563. Bought by another Boston company, Mostyn & Willey Ltd. in 1946, rebuilt and modernised in 1959 by Richards Ironworks Ltd. of Lowestoft. Stranded on Scoby 1963, total loss. Photograph courtesy Mark Stopper collection.

Mace LT 35. Pictured entering Lowestoft harbour in bad weather. Built in 1919, this vessel had various owners before being acquired by Mr. Fred Parkes (Snr.) in the 1940s. Sold to Poland in 1947, returned to Lowestoft in 1949. Photograph courtesy Mark Stopper collection.

Boston Deep Sea Fisheries new offices on the corner of Waveney Road, which were originally occupied by Consolidated Fisheries. Note the prominent crest in the top centre of the building, which is the crest of the town of Boston, Lincolnshire. Photograph courtesy Ernest Graystone.

subsidiaries of the parent firm, while others were condemned to the scrapyard.

One such vessel to enter the Boston fleet, was the *Lord Howe* LT1257. Built in 1917 in the yard of John Chambers Ltd., of Oulton Broad, she was initially ordered and accepted by J. Pitchers and S.W. Rogers as the *Choice Kass* YH571. Her name was changed on acquisition by Lowestoft Herring Drifters Ltd., in 1923. Requisitioned by the Admiralty for war service in 1940 she served with the Royal Navy until 1946, and it was during that period in 1943 when she was purchased by the St. Andrew's Steam Fishing Co. Ltd. Only one year after her return, she was sold for scrap.

Cochrane & Sons Ltd. of Selby constructed the *Lord Barham* LT211 for the Lowestoft Steam Herring Drifters Ltd. She too was sold to the the St. Andrew's company who later sold her to U.N.R.R.A. They put her on charter to a Polish firm. 1949 saw her back in Lowestoft again, where she remained until 1960 before her sale to Belgian shipbreakers.

The *Lord Hood* LT20 was another product of the Selby yard for the same owners. She too saw war service from 1939 until 1945. The St. Andrew's company bought her in 1943, and sold her to Poland in 1947. On being purchased by R.C. Cook, A.W. Easto, and R.H. Colby in 1949, she returned to Lowestoft, where, in 1950 she was sold again to Major Bill Suddaby. The coveted Prunier Herring Trophy was won by the *Lord Hood* on three occasions. In 1952, under Skipper E. Thompson she came home to land 314 crans of herring. The remainder of her seagoing existence was under various ownerships, in 1960 to Ribble Trawlers Ltd., of Fleetwood, then on to Picton Trawlers Ltd. of Milford Haven in 1959 and again later to another owner of which no details are available, before going for scrap in the 1960's.

Another of the eight Lord fleet vessels, again built by the Selby yard of Cochrane & Sons Ltd., was the *Lord Anson* LT344. Delivered to Lowestoft Steam Herring Drifters in 1927, she was sold to the St. Andrew's company in 1943 while she too was serving with the Royal Navy from 1943 to 1946. Her stay with the Boston subsidiary was only until 1947 when she was sold to J.C. Llewellin Trawlers Ltd. of Milford Haven. William Picton (Milford Haven) bought her in 1950 then sold her to Anson Steam Trawlers Ltd. of the same port in 1955. They scrapped her in 1957.

With no fewer than eight different owners, the 96ft. *Lord Rodney* LT390, built at Goole in 1927 was acquired by her second owners, the St. Andrew's company in 1943, and

following the same pattern they sold her in 1946 to Poland where she became the *Eugeniousz* GOY111. Back in Lowestoft in 1949, she reverted to her original name under a new registration number LT79. After twenty-five years service with the firm, she was scrapped in 1976.

From the John Chambers yard in Oulton Broad, the *Lord Suffolk* LT44 entered service in 1929 and was sold to the Boston company in 1943. She was converted to diesel in 1958 when a 335 h.p. 5-cyl Mirrlees Bickerton & Day engine was installed. Her last owners were Kilfrey Trawling Co. Ltd. of Swansea from 1972 until she sailed for the breakers yard in 1976.

After a variety of seven different owners, and a good fishing career, the *Lord Collingwood* LT183 was also scrapped.

Of course, over the years, many more trawlers were added to those above, far too numerous to detail here, culminating in an impressive prominent fleet.

During the war years, very little fishing was done in the North Sea; minefields and other restricted areas prevented access. For five years the fishing grounds there were not disturbed, so on cessation of hostilities fish stocks there were in abundance. Lowestoft was never a distant water port as such. Vessels sailing out of that port were more inclined to work the North Sea, Southern Norway or the South West Approaches. So, when the war finally ended, the North Sea provided a lucrative opportunity, especially as Lowestoft fishermen landed a large variety of species, Dover sole, lemon sole, plaice, monks, turbot, saith, hake, not forgetting cod and haddock.

The boom of the post-war years was greeted with great enthusiasm, and as always the Boston company was not slow in taking advantage. More new trawlers increased their fleet, but their policy of switching trawlers from port to port was not always popular with the crews as it meant a longer absence from home.

A whole new fleet of trawlers were built for Bostons' by Richards Ironworks Ltd. of Lowestoft. The *Twinkling Star* KY347 spent only a few years with the company before being transferred to the Adam Steam Fishing Co. Ltd., who later sold her to Milford Haven. *Boston Mosquito* LT287 was another brief resident which arrived in 1947. Transferred to Sea Nymph Fisheries Ltd. Halifax, N.S. in 1952, she was renamed the *Acadia Pioneer*. She foundered off Port Hood Islands in 1962. The *Boston Spitfire I* LT285, delivered in 1947, also went to the Canadian subsidiary to become *Acadia Fisher*. She later became a total loss when she was wrecked off Canso Straits.

Another ill-fated trawler which the Boston company sold to

Canada was the *Boston Swallow* LT405. She went to British Columbia Packers Ltd. of Vancover B.C. in 1952 and was renamed *Rupert Brand*. Her end came when she was lost after a collision with the Norwegian steamer, *Avenir*. Luckily there were no casualties.

By a curious twist of fate, the Canadian acquisitions, except one, were doomed for disaster. The *Boston Hornet I* LT182 was the only one which survived. Richards of Lowestoft built her for Bostons' in 1952 and without ever fishing out of Lowestoft, she was sold within days of completing her trials to Fishery Products Ltd. of St. Johns, Newfoundland, ending her days as a a training ship to a Fisheries college before going to the breaker's yard in 1967.

Disasters were not by any means unique to Canada. Our fishing industry in this country has also had more than its fair share of adversity as the incidents related below will prove.

BOSTON PIONAIR LOST WITH ALL HANDS

Fishing ports everywhere are no strangers to tragedy or disasters. Accidents and mortalities leave their scars on family life and Lowestoft is no exception.

The 103ft. trawler, *Boston Pionair* LT432 left Lowestoft on 6th. February 1965 in the company of other vessels, one of which was the *Boston Widgeon* (Skipper William Deacon). They were steaming a north-easterly course, and for the next six days they fished from the tail of the Dogger Bank and the Horn Reef. Skipper of the *Boston Pionair*, twenty-five year old, Brian Moyse was accompanied by his father, fifty-nine year old Bert Moyse who was sailing as the ship's cook.

On the evening of Friday 12th February, at 6pm, the BBC broadcast a warning to shipping of gales increasing to Storm Force 10. Both the skippers of the *Widgeon* and *Pionair*, decided to steam S.S.W. At about 7.20pm the *Pionair* was seen by the skipper of *Widgeon* to be steaming in that direction. A little later the *Widgeon* lost all visible contact.

The extremely bad weather persisted throughout the night and at 6.30 on the Sunday morning, while the skipper of the *Widgeon* was talking over the radio to Skipper Moyse, the *Boston Pionair* failed to reply on the word "over". The skipper of the *Boston Widgeon*, then contacted the trawler *Roy Stevens*, and asked her skipper to try to contact the *Pionair*, who after a number of attempts also failed to get any reply. Skipper Deacon of the *Widgeon* assuming that the bad weather had most probably damaged the *Pionair's* aerial, waited until evening thinking by

then the aerial would be repaired, before he again tried to contact the *Pionair*. Still there was no reply, so on the following day, the *Widgeon* reported to the owners that he had lost all contact with the *Pionair*.

The owners waited until 16th February; by then their concern for the vessel's safety was such that they asked Humber Radio to alert all shipping. At about 1.50pm on that day, a lifeboat was reported to have been sighted. This was later retrieved by a French trawler.

An intensive air and sea search was instigated involving two frigates of the Royal Navy, four Shackleton aircraft of the R.A.F., and every available Lowestoft trawler, about twenty in all. The French trawler *Lafayette*, which had picked up the lifeboat, was later boarded by Skipper Victor Crisp of the *Boston Victor*, leader of the trawler search vessels, who identified it as that belonging to the *Boston Pionair*. After a prolonged search 70 miles north-east of Scarborough, the area where the lifeboat was first spotted, no trace was found of the vessel. She was never seen again. Lost with all hands.

Several factors emerged at the inquiry, one regarding "undesirable low stability", due most probably to outdated design and another, watertight doors. However, no blame or criticism was levelled at the owners, neither was there any negligence on anyone's part.

Of the *Boston Pionair's* crew of nine, all except one were married men who left a total of thirteen children, with two of the wives expecting babies. The crew included a father and son, and two others who were brothers. The full crew were: Skipper Brian Moyse (aged twenty-five), Mate, Gordon Beamish (49), Third Hand Michael Lark (21), Chief Engineer, Antony Thurston (33), Second Engineer, Walter Thurston (31), Cook, Bert Moyse (59), Deckhands, John Genery (23), William Stebbing (20) and Michael Lee (27).

Boston Hornet LT 182. The one survivor out of the four Boston vessels transferred to Canada, the other three were all lost. Photograph courtesy P.L.R.S. collection.

Boston Pionair LT 432 seen here entering Lowestoft harbour. Photograph courtesy P.L.R.S. collection.

Boston Comet LT 421. She was lucky to survive the ordeal. Photograph courtesy Maritime Photo Library.

BOSTON COMET 'BATTERED BUT SAFE'

'Battered but safe', blazoned the headline on the front page of the *Eastern Evening News* on 17th January 1968. It signified a comforting end to what might well have been a sinister repeat of the *Boston Pionair* incident.

Badly battered, the 93ft. *Boston Comet* LT421 limped into Lowestoft harbour earlier on that day and berthed in the Waveney Dock. Extensive damage to her super-structure aft of the wheelhouse was convincing evidence of the ordeal the vessel and her crew had endured. Wheelhouse windows were smashed. Interior damage included extensive damage to expensive navigation equipment and radios which the violent seas had ripped off from her bulkheads, on the after deck her lifeboat was missing from its chocks and all lifesaving and safety gear had vanished.

The arrival in port of the 137 tons trawler came just in time to prevent a massive sea and air search which had been organised and was due to begin. The crew, shaken, but thankfully all safe, were able to tell of their nightmare experience.

The vessel had shipped some enormous seas which had torn off the wheelhouse doors and carried away the lifeboat, also sweeping away one of the ship's inflatable life rafts.

Skipper George Outlaw told of the nerve-wracking moments while fishing the White Bank grounds about 220 miles north-east of Lowestoft, when the full fury of the most violent of Neptune's terrible moods struck. As he watched the approach of the largest freak sea he had ever seen he thought his ship could not possibly ride it. "We were dodging in the worst wind and sea I have ever seen", he said "When I saw this huge freak wave bearing down on us I knew we could never ride over it and all we could do was to hang on and hope. It smashed down over our bows and buried us. Over the wheelhouse it came, smashing three windows, the force of the water ripping all the electric, radio and navigation equipment off the bulkheads. The ship was full of water on deck up to her rails but fortunately we did not take any below. The port inflatable life raft was carried away and the other inflated itself on deck". He said they continued dodging until the weather abated then, when it was safe enough, he went ahead and made for home.

For once, a reasonably happy ending, a near tragedy averted; at least that time there was no loss of human life. Structural damage and equipment can be repaired or replaced, all they require is money, but human life is irreplaceable.

What makes a man go to sea for a living, especially fishing? What makes a bird sing? Most certainly it is not the money, I have yet to meet a wealthy retired fisherman. Most of them end up with no more than they started with. And yet there was never any shortage of good hard working men to man our trawlers. A fisherman's life is not for the faint hearted, nervous or squeamish, not just a job it is a calling and for that reason fishermen throughout the land are known as a race apart.

Once he leaves port, he will be away from sixteen to twenty-one days when he will be on call twenty-four hours a day. On reaching the fishing grounds he must be ready to work on deck, in all weather for eighteen hours, hauling the trawl every two hours and gutting fish in between, with only a break of six hours, before returning to duty. The fishing grounds will depend upon the skipper and the owner. He may go to Iceland, Faroes, White Sea, or the Barent Sea, all of which are noted for atrocious weather, gales, severe freezing and ice packs. Fishing will continue at all times unless the weather gets so severe it becomes impossible. During those times he may spend several days *dodging,* which means, the skipper will only maintain just enough way (engine power) on the ship to hold her head to wind. The reason being, he will most probably be facing thirty to forty feet waves and to allow his vessel to go broadside on to the sea could cause her to founder. Another danger he will face is in the freezing conditions when the spray from seas breaking over the ship freezes as it settles on the super-structure. He will then be required, and called out, even if it is his six hours below decks, to chop away the ice, because if it is allowed to accumulate the vessel would become unstable.

Once on board his ship, he is at the beck and call of the Skipper. His word is law. Strikes and malpractices are unknown to him, neither does he have the protection of a trades union. He may be criticized ashore as a boozing rough diamond, but at sea he is a reformed character, obedient, honest and hard working. On returning to port to land their catch, he will have only forty-eight hours respite before sailing again.

The extreme proximity of shipboard life creates for him a lifestyle of comradeship, and his shipmates are his friends. By the very nature of their calling, fishermen are a close knit community. A very close bond exists between all seafaring men, and that comradeship remains with them all their lives.

Should you get chatting to him in a pub, you will find him amicable and polite, he will respect you for what you are. If he had landed a good trip it is most certain he will buy you a pint, if he hasn't, he certainly won't.

Although he may have encountered disasters at sea in the past, you will not hear of those. He considers such things to be merely hazards of the job. But take care, you will not be accepted or included in his circle of close friends; those are people he knows he can trust with his life.

On the whole, those people who choose not to go to sea will not understand him. Therefore when you leave him, it may well be with the impression, "What a strange chap".

In the early days of sail life was even more difficult for the fisherman. Manual labour was required for every job, and living conditions on board were very primitive. With the advent of steam, although the natural elements remained, life was made easier. Steam-powered winches replaced the back-breaking toil of hauling the nets by hand, but although the vessels were larger, the extra space was required for coal bunkering.

More improvements came with diesel power, on board electrics and modern ships. Sir Fred Parkes, the famous Bostonian, who was the principal behind the Boston Deep Sea Fishing Company always with the welfare and safety of his crew members in mind, introduced better living standards on board his vessels. This humane policy was continued by Sir Fred's son Sir Basil Parkes. All his new ships were built with accommodation for all the crew placed in the more comfortable position aft. Smaller cabins replaced the old forward communal living spaces, showers were installed, and later in his larger stern trawlers and freezers, hospital quarters were added, together with recreational space. Both Sir Fred and Sir Basil also insisted on incorporating every new navigation and maritime aid as they appeared on the market.

It is not my intention to create the illusion that life on board trawlers became luxurious, this is certainly not so. The large freezer trawlers did not replace the smaller side trawler. They were built specifically for the long three month trips to the Newfoundland grounds and the Arctic. Side trawlers continued to fish the nearer conventional grounds.

Over the last forty years a fisherman's life has been plagued by all kind of problems: the three Icelandic Cod Wars, when they were forced to work under hazardous conditions were, in themselves perilous. Iceland, claimed first twelve mile, then fifty and shortly after, two hundred mile limits. Our Government conceded. Then there is the European Community, where our fishermen were, and are being, used as pawns in sinister bargaining for other things which might attract more votes.

The men I have spoken of are the finest seamen in the world, whose expertise is paramount. All they ask is to be allowed to go to sea, earn a living and provide your table with the best quality fish available. Instead, most of them have been thrown prematurely on the scrap heap, into enforced idleness to watch helplessly as foreigners are allowed to take our fish and sell it back to you.

At a time when the European Common Fisheries Policy and their scientists were telling us North Sea fish stocks were terribly low, there was an amazing contradiction of terms when on Monday the 5th. July 1971, the Lowestoft trawler *Boston Whirlwind* entered harbour to land her catch.

The vessel, owned by Boston Deep Sea Fishing Co. Ltd., and under the command of Skipper Ian Lace, was the centre-point of excitement as onlookers saw the trawler, deep in the water from the weight of fish she carried. Not only was her fishroom filled to capacity, her decks were also full almost to her rails, a sight never witnessed before in Lowestoft even at the height of trawling's heyday.

Mr. Peter Catchpole, manager for the owners, was quoted as saying, "It is the most amazing catch I have ever seen. Nothing like it has ever been seen at the port before. We have seen drifters returning to port in the past with herring on their decks, but never trawlers. People at the port say they cannot remember anything like it before".

With her decks completely full of fish, Skipper Lace was forced to arrange for a catwalk to be erected over the deck to allow the crew to go forward without treading on fish.

Skipper Lace had sailed on the Sunday and after fishing for seven days had called the Company by radio on the following Saturday to inform them he had on board 2,500 stone of cod. Then he called in again on the Sunday to say he had another 3,500 stone of cod, which apparently had been taken in no more than twenty-four hours fishing. The *Boston Whirlwind*, landed a total of 6,000 stone of cod.

The son of another Lowestoft skipper, Harry Lace, Ian had been a 'Boston' skipper for five years, first in the *Boston Vulcan*, then in the *Boston Scimitar*, before taking command of the *Boston Whirlwind*. Mr. Catchpole described Ian as "one of our great young skippers". When asked where he had caught this record catch, all Skipper Lace would say was "Less than 100 miles from Lowestoft".

An excellent achievement. The *Boston Whirlwind*'s good fortune followed that of her sister ship the *Boston Widgeon* which, on the previous Friday, had landed 2,370 stone of cod which had been taken in only 48 hours. Her skipper, Alex Lincoln, said his catch was made about 70 miles from Lowestoft.

Some of the crew at work on board the Lowestoft Lady. Second right is Malcolm Breach who kindly loaned this photo.

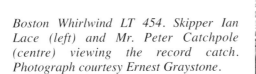

Boston Whirlwind LT 454. Skipper Ian Lace (left) and Mr. Peter Catchpole (centre) viewing the record catch. Photograph courtesy Ernest Graystone.

STERN TRAWLERS FOR LOWESTOFT

Prior to the decimation of our fishing industry, before the so called Common Fisheries Policy was implemented, Boston Deep Sea Fisheries in 1969/70 introduced a new concept of trawling into Lowestoft.

During their trawler operations in Canada, the Boston company had been very impressed by the success of a new design of trawler, of which five such vessels of around 130ft. had been operated by them. They were interested enough to send several of their top skippers out to Canada to sail with the vessels and observe their potential with a view to using that type of trawler in the U.K. The skippers' reports were most favourable and the company continued their project.

In a report in the *Lowestoft Journal* newspaper dated Friday October 24th. 1969, the Chairman of Boston Deep Sea fisheries, Mr. B.A. Parkes, was quoted as saying, "At the present moment our group headquarters technical staff, together with one or two keen members and skippers of our Lowestoft staff and the industrial development unit of the White Fish Authority, whom we have specially commissioned, have nearly completed design of a prototype of stern trawler which we intend to build for our Lowestoft fleet".

It was found this type of trawler, towing her gear from the port and starboard aft gallows, was more easy to handle. More important to the company, the work of the fishermen would not only be less arduous but far safer.

The company put out tenders for the initial building of five stern trawlers and by 1978, in fact on Friday 23rd of June of that year, the same newspaper, under the headline "Boston expansion waits on fishing policy", said, "When the current series of trawlers was finished, Boston Deep Sea Fisheries would have invested £6 million in the port of Lowestoft".

This considerable investment was indeed a courageous venture during a period of great uncertainty. It certainly demonstrated faith in the future of Lowestoft if our Government adopted the fishing industry's call for a 50 miles exclusive limit round the shores of the U.K.

Ten more modern stern trawlers were planned for Lowestoft but the new investment would be held back because of the EEC's, as it was named then, indecision on a Common Fisheries Policy. The fishing industry was prepared to await a satisfactory deal. They were totally united in supporting the resolute stand of the Minister, Mr. John Silkin, in his EEC negotiations.

The Boston company's conservation record had been outstanding and unblemished compared with our EEC partners. It was imperative it included an increase in white fish net mesh size, which Lowestoft had already implemented. However, the EEC proposals on conservation and control were very weak and in practice would only be observed by Britain.

In retrospect, we know now how the EC Common Fisheries Policy has become loaded against the British fishermen. The U.K. contribution of over 60% of European fishery resources went unheeded, all our fishermen got was the thin edge of the wedge.

Boston Sea King LT 265. One of Boston's first new stern trawlers. Photograph courtesy K.W. Kent.

Boston Sea Knight LT 319. Photograph courtesy Mark Stopper collection.

Boston Sea Ranger LT 328. She was lost off south-west Cornwall during the mackerel season. Photograph courtesy Mark Stopper collection.

Leaving Lowestoft the Boston Sea Vixen LT 390 heading for the fishing grounds in 1982. Photograph courtesy John G. Callis.

Boston Sea Gazelle LT 291. This vessel was later renamed the Britannia Gazelle and de-registered when sold to Britannia Marine, who in turn sold the vessel to undisclosed owners. She made news on television when she was escorted into Hull by a Custom & Excise vessel in 1993, who on searching discovered millions of pounds worth of narcotics on board. Photograph courtesy K.W. Kent.

Launched from the slipway of Richards (Shipbuilders) Ltd., in 1978, Boston Sea Stallion LT 293 was named by Margaret Thatcher just prior to her becoming Prime Minister. Photograph courtesy, K.W. Kent.

Mrs. Enid Suddaby wife of Bill Suddaby, managing director of the Boston company photographed with Mr. J.G. Bell, managing director of Richards (Shipbuilders) Ltd., after the launching of the Boston Sea Harrier. Photograph courtesy Ernest Graystone.

One of the larger type of stern trawler was the Boston Sea Harrier LT 418, seen here being fitted out in 1979. Photograph courtesy K.W. Kent.

Boston Sea Dart LT 94. Photograph courtesy Mark Stopper collection.

Boston Sea Sprite LT 247. Sold to Iceland in 1982. Photograph courtesy K.W. Kent.

Boston Sea Fury LT 139. Photograph courtesy Mark Stopper collection.

DETAILS OF TRAWLERS OWNED BY BOSTON D.S.F. IN LOWESTOFT AND GT. YARMOUTH

VESSEL	Reg. No.	Where Built	Gr. Ton.	Length	Notes
Croton	LT 84	Govan 1898	150	100.6ft.	Bought 1941, sold to breakers 1950.
King Charles	LT 157	Grimsby 1899	159	105.7ft.	Bought 1946, sold 1948. Scrapped 1950.
Delhi	LT 111	Beverley 1903	171	105.0ft.	Scrapped 1957.
Blanche	GY 133	Beverley 1907	173	108.5ft.	Bought 1946. Sold to breakers 1952.
Golden Miller	LT 750	Selby 1910	83	83.3ft.	Bought 1952. Sold to breakers 1957.
Eager	LT1166	Selby 1912	102	92.9ft.	Sold 1963 to Accra. Foundered 1972.
Abiding Star	LT 451	Oulton Broad 1917	117	91.8ft.	Bought 1946. Hulked 1947.
Gervais Rentoul	LT 740	Buckie 1917	98	87.3ft.	Bought 1945. Sold 1949. Broke up 1952.
Lord Howe	LT1257	Oulton Broad 1917	75	80.6ft.	Bought 1943. Sold to breakers 1917.
Cairnmor	LT 293	Aberdeen 1918	97	86.2ft.	Bought 1956. Renamed *Welcome Boys* 1960. Scrapped 1966.
Norman Wilson	KY 228	Aberdeen 1918	96	85.2ft.	Bought 1950, sold to breakers 1957.
Accord	LT1247	Aberdeen 1918	96	86.2ft.	Bought 1946/7. War service 1939- 46. Scrapped 1956.
Glow	LT 668	Aberdeen 1918	96	86.2ft.	Bought 1934, sold 1943. Sold to Norway 1946.
Blue Haze	LT 564	Oulton Broad 1919	97	86.2ft.	Bought 1940, sold 1949. Scrapped 1956.
Bow Wave	LT 589	Oulton Broad 1919	97	86.2ft.	Bought 1940. Sold 1949. Scrapped 1957.
Sunnyside Girl	LT 415	Inverness 1919	97	86.2ft.	Bought 1944. Sold to Norway 1946.
Mace	KY 224	Aberdeen 1919	57	86.2ft.	Bought 1945/46. Sold to Poland 1947.
George Baker	LT1253	Aberdeen 1919	96	86.2ft.	Bought 1944. Sold 1947. Sold to breakers 1955.
Copious	KY175	Oulton Broad 1919	96	86.2ft.	Bought 1945/46. War service 1940-45. Sold to Bloomfields and became *Ocean* YH296. Scrapped 1955..
Genious	FY748	Bowling 1919	96	86.2ft.	Bought 194?. War service 1939-45. Sold 1947. Lost 1956.
Twinkling Star	PD433	Hull 1920	95	86.2ft.	Bought 1945/46. War service 1939-45. Scrapped 1960.
Acorn	KY194	Aberdeen 1920	96	86.2ft.	Bought 1954, sold to breakers 1975.
Plough	KY232	Flint 1920	95	86.1ft.	Bought 1945/46. Lost at sea 1948.
Spes Aurea	LT72	Flint 1920	95	86.1ft.	Bought 194?, sold 1946.
Feaco	LT207	Aberdeen 1924	123	90.0ft.	Bought 1950. Sold to Ghana 1967.
Lord Hood	LT 20	Selby 1925	92	85.2ft.	Bought 1943, sold 1947, bought back again 1950, sold 1958.
Lord Barham	LT 211	Selby 1925	92	85.2ft.	Bought 1943. Sold 1947. Sold to breakers 1960.
Lord Anson	LT 344	Selby 1927	100	88.3ft.	Bought 1943. Sold 1947. Sold to breakers 1957.
Lord Rodney	LT 390	Goole 1928	104	96.0ft.	Bought 1943. Sold 1947. Sold 1976.
Lord Suffolk	LT 44	Oulton Broad	115	92.0ft.	Bought 1943. Sold 1946. Sold to breakers 1976.
Comrades	LT 403	Selby 1928	118	92.0ft.	Built as steam drifter, converted to diesel 1955. Sold 1967.

Ocean Lifebuoy	YH 29	Aberdeen 1929	131	94.3ft.	Bought 1955, sold to breakers 1973.
Ocean Lux	YH 84	Aberdeen 1930	125	94.3ft.	Bought 1955, sold to breakers 1975.
Kirkey	LT 225	Colchester	111	93.2ft.	Bought 1946. Stranded on Scroby 1963, total loss.
Dawn Waters	LT 90	Yarmouth 1930	116	92.3ft.	Bought 1954. Converted from steam to diesel 1954. Sold 1962.
Lord Keith	LT 181	Goole 1930	116	92.3ft.	Bought 1943. Sold to Cyprus 1975
Lord Collingwood	LT 183	Goole 1930	116	92.3ft.	Bought 1943. Sold 1947. Sold to breakers 1970.
Kindred Star	LT 177	Oulton Broad 1930	120		Sold 1965.
Willing Boys	LT 737	Oulton Broad 1930	138	98.0ft.	Bought 1974, sold to breakers 1977.
Willa	LT 43	Lowestoft 1937	81	75.3ft.	Bought 1946. Sold 1947.
Celita	LT 236	Lowestoft 1939	78	75.1ft.	Bought 1946. Sold 1947. Sold to breakers 1970.
Betty Leslie	LT 347	Lowestoft 1943	115	96.0ft.	Bought 1960. Was LK497. Sold 1973. Scrapped 1976.
William Rhodes Moorhouse	LO 496	Oulton Broad 1944	112	88.5ft.	Bought 1948. Sold 1967. Sprang a leak in Southern Irish Sea, total loss 1968.
Firsby	GY 494	Plymouth 1946	117	96.4ft	Bought 1951. Sold to Agadir 1962.
Harrowby	GY 531	Totnes 1946	122	94.8ft	Bought 1951. Sold 1952.
Parkfield	LT 290	Colchester 1946	120	93.2ft.	Bought 1948. Rebuilt 1959. Sold 1967.
Quiet Waters	LT 279	Charlestown 1946	123	92.0ft.	Bought 1951. Sold to Casablanca 1964.
Boston Spitfire	LT 285	Lowestoft 1947	147	96.7ft.	Trans. to Canada 1953. Became *Acadia Fisher*. Wrecked Canso Straits, 1961. Total loss.
Boston Mosquito	LT 287	Lowestoft 1947	147	96.7ft	Trans. to Halifax N.S. 1952. Became *Acadia Pioneer* later *Arctic Fisher*. Foundered off Port Hood Islands 1962.
Starlit Waters	LT 97	Lowestoft 1947	113	92.9ft.	Bought 1952. Sold to Casablanca 1964.
Dauntless Star	LT 371	Selby 1948	133	96.8ft.	Bought 1951. Sold to Canada 1951 became *Red Diamond*.
Sunlit Waters	LT 377	Selby 1948	133	96.8ft.	Bought 1952, became *Boston Swift*. trans. to Canada 1954, sold again in 1957 to Aberdeen as *Swiftburn* A143, bought by Star Drift Fishing Co. Lowestoft, 1958, (a Boston Company) became *Dauntless Star*. Trans. to Hull 1968. Sold back to Lowestoft 1971. Sold to Gulf area 1977.
Boston Comet	LT 421	Lowestoft 1949	157	102.3ft.	Sold to Canada 1952, became Blue Comet. Stranded at St. Pierre 1954, total loss.
Boston Swallow	LT 405	Lowestoft 1949	163	102.3ft.	Sold to British Columbia 1952. Lost after collision 1955.
Boston Hornet	LT 182	Lowestoft 1950	98	82.0ft.	Sold within days of builders trials to Canada, became *Zilik*, later fishery training ship. Scrapped 1967.
W.F.P.	LT 144	Lowestoft 1950	112	87.1ft.	Bought 1952 as *Boston Hunter*. Sold to Chile 1958. Wrecked on rocks, Corral Bay 1969, lost.
St. Luke	LT 156	Hessle 1950	114	84.5ft.	Sold 1961.
Boston Lancaster	LT 713	Aberdeen 1952		124.7ft.	Launched as *Princess Royal* FD175 later *Acadia Heron*, 1967 *Boston Lancaster*. Sold 1973.

Boston Sea Hawk	LT 430	Hessle 1953	180	102.2ft.	Sold to Milford Haven 1956, then to Aberdeen 1957 as A174, then Isle of Man, to Fleetwood 1979, converted to stern trawler 198?
Boston Victor I	LT 433	Hessle 1953	188	102.2ft.	Sold 1958. Total loss 197?
Boston Pegasus	LT 58	Lowestoft 1954	166	103.0ft.	Sold 1972. Went aground Whitley Bay 1977, broke up.
Diadem	LT 59	Lowestoft 1954	166	103.0ft.	Sold 1973. Scrapped 1979.
Boston Spitfire II	LT 218	Lowestoft 1955	166	103.0ft.	Sold to Sri Lanka 1965, as *Ishwary*.
Lowestoft Lady	LT 247	Lowestoft 1955	166	103.0ft.	Sold to Sri Lanka 1966.
Boston Vulcan	LT 475	Hessle 1955	182	102.2ft.	Bought 1963. Was *St. Hilda* HL25
Princess Anne	LT 740	Beverley 1955		139.7ft.	1974 renamed Boston Wellington. Sold 1974. Scrapped 1975.
Boston Seafoam	FD 42	Hessle 1956	398	138.8ft.	Sold 1974.
Boston Valetta	LT 256	Aberdeen 1956	238	111.0ft.	Renamed *Acadia Fin-Fare* 1961, back as *Boston Valetta* 1968. Sold 1971, scrapped 1976.
Boston Pionair	LT 432	Lowestoft 1956	166	103.0ft.	Foundered in North Sea, total loss, 1965.
Boston Harrier	LT 76	Aberdeen 1956	238	111.0ft.	Launched as *Acadia Snowbird*. Sold 1972. Scrapped 1976.
Boston Viking	LT 510	Hessle 1956	174	94.1ft.	Sold to Ireland 1973. Returned to B.D.S.F. 1974. Sold again 1982.
Hawfinch	FD 114	Hessle 1956	314	127.5ft	Sold 1979.
Boston Herald	LT 222	Lowestoft 1956	166	103.0ft.	Trans. to St. Andrew's, Hull Sold to Mrs Heather Anderson of Caister on Sea 1970, renamed 1971, *Flying Duchess*, sold to Nigeria 1972 as *Wushishi Conquest*.
Boston Invader	FD 161	Aberdeen 1956	407	153.5ft.	Launched as *Red Rose* LO36, renamed *Boston Invader* 1972, later *Inverlochy*. Sold 1978.
Boston Defender	FD 163	Aberdeen 1957	391	139.6ft.	Launched as *Captain Riou* LO72, renamed *Boston Defender* 1972, converted to oil rig tender 1976. Sold 1978.
Boston Trident	LT 474	Hessle 1957		102.2ft.	Bought 1963. Sold 1972. Scrapped 1979.
Boston Halifax I	LT 355	Lowestoft 1958	197	106.4ft.	Sold to France 1963 as *Chipeau* CC3375.
Boston Seallow	LT 323	Lowestoft 1958	197	106.4ft.	Sold to France 1963 as *Le Martinet* CC3855.
Boston Arrow	LT 113	Lowestoft 1959	197	106.4ft.	Sold to France 1963 as *Avocette* CC3886.
Boston Coronet	GY 596	Lowestoft 1959	199	108.6ft.	Re-registered as LT495 in 1963. Sold to Mazara del Vallo 1980 as *Lidia Prima*.
Boston Corsair	LT 148	Lowestoft 1959	135	92.2ft.	Converter to oil rig stand-by 1962. Fishing Reg'n cancelled 1975.
Boston Scimitar	LT 100	Lowestoft 1959	135	92.2ft.	Converted to oil rig stand-by 1977, de-registered.
Highland Lady	LT 429	Beverley 1959	211	102.0ft.	Was A347. Renamed *Boston Javelin* 1964. Sold to Greece 1972.
Hazelhead	A 364	Beverley 1959	174	103.0ft.	Renamed *Boston Hunter II* LT460 1963. Sold to Norway 1971.
Woodside	A 365	Aberdeen 1959	190	101.1ft.	Renamed *Boston Victor II* LT473. Sold 1975.
Valiant Star	LT 277	Lowestoft 1959	160	97.2ft.	Sold 1972.

Universal Star	A 344	Gateshead 1959	242	103.9ft	Re-reg'd. LT479 1964. Sold 1968.
Boston Argosy	LT 364	Lowestoft 1960	195	106.8ft.	De-registered 1975.
Boston Comet II	LT 183	Brightlingsea 1960	137	93.6ft	To oil rig stand-by work and de-registered 1976.
Boston Hornet II	LT 173	Brightlingsea 1960	131	91.6ft.	To oil rig stand-by and de-reg'd. 1976.
Boston Provost	LT 247	Lowestoft 1960	200	106.8ft.	Scrapped 1982.
Boston Wasp	LT 238	Aberdeen 1960	300	115.0ft.	Was GY639. Sold for conversion into cargo ship.
Suffolk Kinsman	LT 397	Lowestoft 1960	202	106.6ft.	Bought 1974 renamed *Boston Kinsman*.
Boston Trystar	GY 210	Aberdeen 1960	434	139.8ft.	Launched as *Captain Foley* LO33 renamed *Boston Trystar* 1972. Sold 1976.
Boston Shackleton	LT 714	Portsmouth 1960	310	115.5ft.	Sold to Colne Shipping 1982.
Boston Buccaneer	LT 157	Lowestoft 1961	165	93.5ft.	Sold 1975.
Boston Widgeon	LT 427	Lowestoft 1961	165	93.5ft.	Sold 1973.
Boston Beaver	LT 445	Lowestoft 1962	165	93.5ft.	De-reg'd. and trans. to oil rig stand-by 1977.
Boston Whirlwind	LT 454	Lowestoft 1962	165	93.5ft.	Converted to oil rig stand-by 1979.
Boston Islander	FD 263	Den Holder 1962	102	85.0ft.	Bought 1973. Sold 1976.
Boston Wayfarer	LT 508	Hessle 1965	174	94.1ft.	Sold to South Africa 1981.
Boston Viscount	LT 509	Hessle 1965	174	94.1ft.	Sold 1983.
Boston Defiant	LT 517	Hessle 1966	174	94.1ft.	Launched as *Deeside* LT517 renamed *Boston Defiant* 1973. Complete with B.D.S.F.
Boston Jaguar	LT 463	Hessle 1966	174	94.1ft.	Sold to South Africa 1981.
Roy Stevens	LT 271	Lowestoft 1971	202	106.6ft.	Bought 1974 and renamed *Boston Aztec*. Sold 1980.
Boston Sea Dart	LT 94	Renfrew 1972	312	109.3ft.	Sold 1983.
Boston Sea Sprite	LT 247	Berwick 1972	311	109.3ft.	Sold 1982.
Boston Sea Fury	LT 139	Renfrew 1973	312	109.1ft.	Sold to Iceland.
Boston Mariner	LT 378	Lowestoft 1974	202	106.6ft.	Sold to South Africa 1980.
Boston Halifax	GY 321	Goole 1975	387	123.11ft	Remained with Bostons.
Boston Sea King	LT 265	Paull 1976	171	84.10ft	Sold to South Africa 1983.
Boston Sea Knight	LT 319	Paull 1976	171	84.10ft	Converted to oil rig stand-by 1984.
Boston Sea Ranger	LT 382	Paull 1976	171	84.10ft	Lost off S.W. Cornwall 1977.
Boston Sea Vixen	LT 390	Gt. Yarmouth 1978	189	86.2ft	Converted to oil rig stand-by 1984.
Boston Sea Cobra	LT 290	Gt. Yarmouth 1978	189	86.2ft	Converted to oil rig stand-by 1984.
Boston Sea Gazelle	LT 291	Gt. Yarmouth 1978	190	86.2ft	Converted to oil rig stand-by 1984.
Boston Sea Stallion	LT 293	Gt. Yarmouth 1978	190	86.2ft	Converted to oil rig stand-by 1984.
Boston Sea Harrier	LT 418	Gt. Yarmouth 1979	313	109.0ft	Complete service with B.D.S.F.

ACCOLADE FOR SKIPPER

It was in October 1974 when the *Boston Argosy* developed engine trouble in severe and worsening weather conditions. She radioed the *Boston Sea Fury* which was fifty miles away, asking to be taken in tow. The skipper of the *Boston Sea Fury*, Victor Crisp, who was fishing at the time, immediately gave orders for her gear to be hauled, then set a course for the disabled vessel.

Weather conditions deteriorated and by the time Skipper Crisp reached the casualty, there was a Force 8 gale, a heavy swell and snow squalls. It is sometimes very difficult to get a towline on board a vessel under normal conditions, but Skipper Crisp managed to get the *Boston Argosy* secured under tow quickly. Unfortunately after only two hours the towline parted. The gale force wind had by then increased to Force 9 and at times gusting even higher. They were facing 25 ft. to 30 ft. high waves and a strong southerly tide was running.

Visibility was down to 400 yards adding severely to the difficulty re-connecting the tow. It was four hours before they started the tow again. The ships could only proceed at about 2.5 knots taking 50 hours for them to cover the 220 miles back to Lowestoft.

Skipper Crisp was well known in Lowestoft for his gallant exploits. He had been involved on several occasions when vessels were in trouble, now two years after the *Boston Argosy* incident he was presented with a silver rose bowl in recognition of his outstanding seamanship and skills. The award was made by the Secretary of State for Trade, Mr. Peter Shore. Presenting the bowl...officially known as "a piece of plate", on behalf of the Department of Trade, Mr. Cecil Creber, a principal officer of the London Marine Survey District, said, "The operation had called for skill, seamanship and bravery. It was true to the spirit of seamanship and bravery which is maintained in the port of Lowestoft". In reply Skipper Crisp commented, "No man in charge of a ship can do it without his crew and I had a particularly good crew at that time".

Boston Deep Sea Fisheries' prosperity in Lowestoft was the result of excellent management and the employment of the best skippers, and as the company began to wind down they remained in Lowestoft until the very end in the early 1980's, when the company finally disposed of all its commitments. The firm as we all knew it no longer existed. A very sad day for the fishing industry in Lowestoft.

Chapter Six

Canada

In 1952, Boston Deep Sea Fisheries decided to explore distant horizons for further expansion of their interests. Mr. Basil Parkes already had dealings in the past with Canadian companies. Now the Boston company was ready and interested to establish itself on the Canadian east coast.

Their opportunity arose when it became known that a small firm of salt fish curers run by two brothers, Fletcher and Ab Smith of Halifax, Nova Scotia, were very keen to develop their business in a wider area of fish processing. The Smith brothers did not have the necessary capital to invest in trawlers or the expertise to indulge in this venture, so an equal partnership was formed between Bostons' and the Smith brothers, the Boston company putting up the capital to buy the much needed trawlers. A new company was formed under the name of Acadia Fisheries Ltd., Acadia being the old name for Nova Scotia.

During the first year of trading, the new company landed 7,000,000 lbs of fish and within ten years this had increased to a colossal 24,000,000 lbs. Even so, to venture into this business was indeed very risky for Bostons' in an area notorious for its bad weather and Arctic conditions, where the sea is frozen over during winter months.

Mr. A.B. Wilbraham went over to Canada to represent the Boston company's interests, remaining there for the next ten years.

Money for the new plant began to run out in 1954 and more capital was urgently required. To raise more funds, it was decided to offer non voting preference shares, of which the Boston company held the greater proportion. The Smith brothers then began to look for new investors to back them in a take-over bid against Bostons. Both sides agreed to submit sealed bids which proved unsuccessful for the Smith brothers, and the Canadian company thus became another part of the Boston conglomerate.

Production increased and new larger trawlers, more adaptable to fishing off the Canadian east coast were purchased. New lines in frozen fish were developed and sold under the Snowbird label. Canada at that time was not highly populated so the United States became the company's biggest outlet, taking 80% of its total production.

Although Mr. Wilbraham returned to England in 1962 to take charge of the United Towing Company, a firm owning tugs and cargo vessels which operated from Hull, the Canadian company, because of the extremely large investment made into it, went on to become the largest producer of fish in eastern Canada, with a fleet of ten trawlers.

The first new stern trawler to enter service for the Acadia Fishing Co., was the *Acadia Albatross*. Built in Nova Scotia by Ferguson Industries Ltd., she arrived from the builders in 1965. This vessel, 151ft. long, a beam of 33ft. and with a gross tonnage of 800, proved very successful, consistently outfishing the side trawlers in the Acadia fleet. Spurred on by her encouraging performance, the company ordered four more stern trawlers of similar tonnage, length and design.

The *Acadia Thunderbird* and *Acadia Gannet* were completed in 1968, both powered by a Ruston 1,650 hp eight cylinder diesel engine, driving a controllable pitch propeller which gave them a speed of 11.5 Knots. Their fishroom capacity was 400,000 lbs and on deck a trawl winch could take 1,200 fathoms of one inch diameter wire warp. They carried a crew of twenty. Both vessels made good landings, also outfishing their counterparts of similar size.

So impressed were they by their performance when all four new stern trawlers were in operation, the company seriously considered whether ships of a similar design might be built for Fleetwood. Two of the Boston company's top Fleetwood skippers, Skipper Bill Rawcliffe of the *Boston Phantom* and Skipper Bill Bridge of the *Captain Fremantle*, were sent over to Canada to make a trip in one of the stern trawlers to assess her fishing abilities. After a very favourable report by the two skippers, the company did later order vessels of similar design for their U.K. based fleets.

In September 1956, the *Acadia Snowbird* A45 was returned to the U.K. Built as the *Boston Britannia* by the Lewis shipyard of Aberdeen, this trawler had not previously operated from any U.K. port. Her sister ship, the *Acadia Fin-Fare*, also returned and went to Lowestoft. She later fished out of Grimsby as the *Boston Valetta*.

Those Canadian subsidiaries whose attributes to profitability created confidence for future progress, encouraged the Boston company to plough more investment into them. A new wharf was built, together with a new factory, designed to meet the highest of Canadian standards. They also built a new efficient fish meal and oil factory.

Things certainly were going very well for the Canadian subsidiary and their employees until, towards the end of 1970 disagreements between two trade unions caused great upheavals

Acadia Heron, formerly the Princess Royal FD 176, seen here in St. Johns, Newfoundland. She later returned to the U.K. and was renamed Boston Lancaster LT 713. Photograph courtesy P.L.R.S. collection.

Boston Swift, alongside the jetty outside the Boston Company's factory. Note the icing on the vessel's rigging and super-structure. Photograph courtesy Steve Pulfrey.

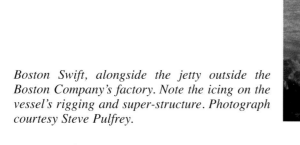

and disruption. The trouble centred on the isolated ports of Canso and Mulgrave in Nova Scotia. The British Columbia based United Fishermen and Allied Workers Union demanded recognition as the main bargaining agent of the industry. The Acadia company would only recognise the Canadian Food and Allied Workers Union.

The U.F.A.W. Union was desperately trying to gain a foothold in the huge east coast fishing industry, but employers were suspicious of their alleged sinister Communist leanings and their militant leaders. The culmination of all those problems came early in 1971 when a strike was called. In an area dependent on fishing it seriously affected the local economy and caused much personal hardship, as over 230 trawlermen, several hundred inshore fishermen and almost 800 factory workers were made idle.

Although the United and Allied Workers Union never succeeded in gaining recognition, more complications arose by legislation passed during that winter. The new Canadian Trades Union Act was passed which specified that no organisation had the right to represent fishermen.

Half the company's trawler fleet had been forced to lay up. Long periods of tension which had developed into stone throwing and boat burning, together with injunctions, had torn the town apart. Ironical really, when one considers the Acadia plant and vessels were the principal support of a fifty mile stretch of coastline, and at a time when prospects for the fishing industry had never looked so good.

One summer afternoon in the same year, at 4pm, the parent company announced that the Acadia company of Canada had ceased to exist. The formal announcement was accompanied by words of deep regret from Great Britain that the actions of the United Fishermen and Allied Workers Union had led to the closure of Boston's two plants in Nova Scotia. In terms of money, it had cost Boston Deep Sea Fisheries over £1,000,000. All their Canadian based vessels were either sold or returned to join the company's home fleet.

They were not alone in their unhappy experiences, joining now, other large companies who had suffered a similar fate in Canada. The Ross Group, Birds Eye and Cosalt had also found difficulties and had been forced to withdraw their business activities there.

Some of the vessels which sailed for Acadia Fisheries were:

Acadia Thunderbird *Acadia Fisher*
Acadia Gannet *Acadia Fin-Fare*
Acadia Albatross *Acadia Snowbird*
Acadia Pioneer *Acadia Seahawk*
Acadia Neptune *Acadia Cormorant*
Acadia Gull

Chapter Seven
The Cod Wars and the EEC

It can be said that 1959 was the year when the decline of the British fishing industry first began. Iceland had been testing the possibilities of claiming an extension of her territorial waters.

Their excuse was that the Icelandic Government was seriously concerned for the fish stocks of the waters around their island, claiming that British trawlers among others, with their new modern vessels and improved fishing methods, were contributing to the grounds being over-fished. There was some truth in their claim, but the problem could easily have been resolved by introducing conservation methods. Indeed, British fishermen have always been aware and very conscious of the need for conservation; it was indeed necessary and to their advantage to do so. Experiments were already in progress on different ways to conserve fish stocks, of which mesh sizes, was just one.

The Icelandic Government's first action was to claim an exclusive twelve miles limit where all foreign vessels would be prevented from taking fish. Britain quite rightly strongly objected, and British fishermen continued to make their trips to those grounds. Iceland replied by sending her small gunboats in an attempt to police their newly declared twelve miles limit. Thus the first 'Cod War' had commenced. The Royal Navy was called in to protect British fishing vessels.

Consideration here must be taken of the fact that Russia was at that time considered a serious threat to the security of the Western World, and Iceland, mainly for her own protection, had agreed to American and United Nations bases being established there. When they realised their attempts to control the fishing situation were a failure, they played their trump card, and threatened to close all Allied Bases in their country.

The very idea struck fear into the Americans who knew this would weaken Western defences against Russia. Considerable pressure was put on the British Government to reconsider their objection. Of course, the British Government have on several occasions been noted for their policy of appeasement, so they began discussions with Iceland who now thought they were the masters. No concessions for Great Britain were forthcoming so our Government meekly conceded to Icelandic demands.

British trawlers continued to fish the waters outside of the twelve mile limit already imposed, but again in 1972, elated with their previous achievement, Iceland again pushed out her limits,

this time to fifty miles. Again, Great Britain protested and referred the matter to the International Court of Justice. Although the Court found in Britain's favour, Iceland refused to accept the jurisdiction of the Court.

The following year 1973, the Icelandic Government issued a statement saying all British vessels must withdraw to the fifty miles limit. They intended, they said, to enforce their new claim with gunboats, and any British trawlers within the fifty mile limit would risk having their trawls cut away. They had by so doing inadvertently declared the second 'Cod War'. Our vessels ignoring the Icelandic directive continued to fish within the newly claimed limit, and in so doing, over sixty trawlers lost their trawls in that way. The Royal Navy was again called in to protect British interests, but mostly acted as observers. To be fair to the Navy they did on a few occasions intervene and force the Icelandic gunboats away. But on the whole, our trawler companies were obliged to use their own ships to sheer off the gunboats in order that some might be able to fish.

Later the Royal Navy was withdrawn while talks were being held in London, but by 1974 our Government again instituted a policy of appeasement. Accepting the Icelandic claim to a fifty mile limit in return for 139 British registered trawlers being allowed to fish within those limits, but allowed only a token, total annual catch of 130,000 tons. This agreement was to stand for only two years.

By the middle of 1975, things again got seriously out of hand when Iceland had the audacity to claim a ridiculous 200 miles limit. This announcement was made by Icelandic Fisheries Minister, Mr. Matthias Bjarnarson, who said the order would come into force on 15th. October 1975. The Royal Navy was sent back to Iceland to protect British trawlers against the Icelandic policy of trawl cutting. Thus 'Cod War 3' began.

Unable to contain the situation themselves, the Icelanders saw our vessels making trips, with some difficulty I may add, but never-the-less making trips. Iceland resorted once more to their tried and trusted weapon, the N.A.T.O. bases. Now they demanded recognition of their new 200 miles limit or N.A.T.O. must leave the base at Keflavic. Our Government again succumbed to foreign pressures.

Feelings in Iceland were by then running very high against the British, and things came to a head when they broke off diplomatic relations with Great Britain. On the 31st. May 1976, N.A.T.O. called a meeting which was to be held in Oslo, Norway between the Foreign Ministers of Britain and Iceland. A diabolical agreement was reached, allowing only 50,000 tons of fish to be taken from so called Icelandic waters. Only twenty-four trawlers, from a register of ninety-three would be allowed to fish at any one time. The agreement was to last for only six months. On expiration on the 1st December 1976, it was never renewed.

It is debatable whether the British Government backed down too easily, or whether they should they have taken a more determined, stronger stance. More than likely it is true, they did back down much too easily. Surely they should have realised, Iceland would have sacrificed their own safety by enforcing their threat of closing the N.A.T.O. bases.

Furthermore, such a small country as Iceland, lightly populated, whose whole economy depends exclusively on fish could easily have been stopped in her tracks by other means. We were by then a member of the European Economic Community. Could not sanctions have been imposed or were they perhaps preparing us for the reduction of our fishing fleets? It may seem to some, in retrospect, perhaps they were.

A little more thought, and more forthright actions, might well have saved our once proud and great fishing industry, instead of creating, bankruptcies, unemployment and much hardship to a hard working, honest and courageous workforce who deserved better.

THE COMMON MARKET

Great Britain's entry into the European Community, was a serious disaster to the fishing industry. We suddenly found ourselves being dictated to by Eurocrats. A Common Fisheries Policy was imposed upon us, restricting our own historic rights.

The European Community always worked in favour of foreign interests, while British fishermen were hopelessly penalised. Sovereignty over our own waters was stolen from us, agreed to by the Government. Licences and quotas were foisted on us. No longer were we free to come and go as we pleased. Our fishermen struggled to survive as they watched foreign vessels stealing our fish. The Irish, Dutch and French did extremely well out of the C.F.P. mostly at our expense while the British fishing industry was being decimated.

At the beginning of 1978, the remains of our trawler fleets were forced to go further afield in their attempts to earn a living, the Norway Coast, White Sea and Greenland, even to the distant Canadian grounds, while foreigners took our fish from our own backyard. Meanwhile at home, as we waited for the E.E.C. to strike a deal with Norway, our industry was being torn apart.

When a deal was made with Norway it was most disappointing and more British trawlers disappeared from the fishing scene. Later both Norway and Russia declared a 200 mile limit.

Many British fishermen fought and died in two World Wars for the freedom of Europe. They served in minesweepers, the most dangerous branch of the Royal Navy. The Patrol Service, as it was known, taking part in every campaign, lost more men and ships than any other section of the Navy. Surely they deserved better.

Sir Basil Parkes O.B.E. with his wife Maisie, and sons, Fred (left) and Neil (right) photographed here in happier times at the launching of one of the Company's new stern trawlers. Photograph courtesy, Walter Fussey & Son.

Chapter Eight

Conclusions

Sir Fred Parkes could never in his wildest dreams have visualised the extent to which his empire would grow.

From his early humble beginnings in Boston Lincolnshire, to Knighthood and world renown. The small fleet of steam trawlers operating from the Lincolnshire port was to develop into the largest privately owned fishing company in the world, belonging to a company, entirely family owned.

First under Sir Fred's control, its successful operations were continued by his son Sir Basil Parkes and expanded, taking over one company after another, until they owned fifty-six subsidiaries.

After the shabby treatment of Sir Fred Parkes by the then Boston Corporation in 1923, he began moving his trawlers to other ports, and by 1926 he had left the town, lock, stock and barrel, to re-establish in Fleetwood, where he was prominent in that town's development over the years. He might well have done the same for Boston, Lincolnshire, where all that remains of a once promising fishing industry is a few tiny shellfish craft, struggling to survive.

The Boston Deep Sea Fishing and Ice Co. Ltd., opened offices and plant, in Hull, Grimsby, Lowestoft, Canada and many other places. Everywhere they soon became prominent in fishing affairs. The company on liquidation, before reforming under their new title, Boston Deep Sea Fisheries Ltd., employed some 4,800 people either ashore or afloat. That figure does not take into account the vast number of others for whom employment was provided indirectly, in ship building, repairing, and many other ancillaries.

Eventually, it would seem, the proud Boston company was forced to accept the fact that, our fisheries, our rights and our freedom have been stolen from us by our new European masters. The British fishing industry, manned by hard working, loyal, experienced and expert seamen were snubbed, insulted and embarrassed by Europe with the consent of our own Government.

Those facts, together with the three 'Cod Wars', that should never have been, contributed totally to the demise and decimation of our once proud fishing fleet and a great company. There can be no doubt, had fishing been encouraged instead of sacrificed, it would today have been a great asset to our economy, providing employment for many and at the same time preserving a reserve fleet and men, should ever our Country be called upon to defend herself again.

SOME OF THE BOSTON COMPANY'S TOP SKIPPERS

A trawler, no matter how modern or well equipped she may be, is only as good as her skipper. It is he who provides the profit or loss of a vessel for its owners. Over the years the Boston Deep Sea Fisheries was most fortunate in attracting the best men to command their ships and below are the names of many of those fine skippers, names which to a number of older members of the fishing industry will, I'm sure, hold nostalgic memories of friends, of trips, and a era now gone.

A. Quantrill	W. Rawcliffe	H. McMillan	R. Wright
J.L. Cossey	W. Barnard	J. Stevens	R. Rawcliffe
B. Wharam	A. Hollington	W. Balls	W. Bridges
M. Raven	I. Lace	R. Studd	E. Ellan
T. Smith	G. Beamish	K. Morgan	G. Wilson
A. Jenson	E. Grans	J. Kirby	L. Long
A. Jenner	R. Beamish	W. Nutten	P. Meen
D. Fletcher	C. Newton	W. Anderson	R. Richards
D. Brown	R. Harris	R. Evens	D. Sherriff
V. Crisp	J. Williams	H. Chantler	W. Cosey
J. Kelly	J. Quantrill	G. DeBlock	W. Beamish
E. Grant	A. Vickers	D. Smith	G. Wilson
T. Whitcombe	A. Dennison	E. Hollington	B. Turner
R. Kluzwiak	C. Scott	C. Jennings	P. Hollington
F. Grant	A. Tenner	T.B. Evens	J. Rawcliffe
A. Harvey	A.E. Hall	G. Outlaw	H. Muttitt
R. Westgate	M. Hough	D. Hunt	P. Wierman
R. Prior	G. Eddoms	J. Bridge	P. Craven
J. Aldous	N. Delf	E. Fieldsend	L. Ayers
J. Reader	V. Holmes	W. Mullender	J. Tomlinson
H. Pook	K. Hawkridge	C. Evens	H. Whitelam
W. Barker	J. Quinn	A. Lincoln	G. Newell
C. Townsend	M. Jensen	H. Kristensen	E. Dam
D. Fletcher	G. Jonassen	H. Dam	J. Reeder
J. Oakes	W. Sandford	A. Buschini	P. Hames
A. Brown	G. Downs	K. Reynolds	A. Ruddock
D. O'Connor	P. Blaney	B.McAvoy	G. Draper
K. Hames	J. Bowie	B. Wright	J. Betty
H. Dingle	K. Hames	C. Pook	R. Ford
A. Webster	A. Holmes	V. Crisp Jnr.	A. Elder
A. Riby	J. Jobson	H. Gander	A. James

V. Holmes   T. Cossey   D. Hunt   L. Long
B. Keable   E. Thompson   P. Prior   B. Moyse
S. Ebernezersson

Looking back over the years at some of the quotes from Newspapers and Fishing Journals.

Cod sells for £21 a kit on Fleetwood market. Top prices are also paid for plaice, haddocks and the small amount of hake available. The middle water trawler *Boston Invader* lands 114 kits of roker and this made over £16 a kit. She grosses £6,209.

Norton Queen's Lowestoft record lasted just three days. *Boston Coronet* has now pushed the record for ships under 100ft. up to £6,067 with a 3,983st. catch, mainly of plaice. Skipper Jimmy Barnard took the vessel to sea for 11 days.

Boston Kestrel lands 1,998 kits from a 27 day trip to the Icelandic waters. Skipper W. Nutten lands to the Hull market and grosses £21,002.

The stern trawler *Boston Blenheim* becomes the second vessel to top £20,000 at Fleetwood. She worked the North Cape off Iceland before returning with 1,781 kits, mainly cod to gross £20,002.

The Boston Group switches the stern trawler *Boston Beverley* from Grimsby to Fleetwood. Skipper Bob Rawcliffe is expected to take over the ship at Grimsby. Fleetwood will in turn lose the side trawler *Boston Phantom* which is switching to Grimsby. *Penzance Pegasus* moves from Newlyn to Milford Haven where she will be commanded by Skipper Joe Utting. Built for Boston in 1954, she worked from Lowestoft before moving to Newlyn.

Boston's Trawler *St. Chad* returns to Hull from the Icelandic grounds with a £12,768 catch of 1,176 kits plus the warp cutting gear of the gunboat *Aegir*. The cutter was passed on to the Royal Navy for examination and was found to be like a two pronged grapnel, with blades welded inside of either arm.

Two trawlers are battered by freak waves, some 50ft. high and 100 yards long, off the coast of Iceland. The Fleetwood trawler *SSAFA* and the Hull trawler *Kingston Almandine* are badly damaged.

The Esberg, Denmark seiner *Martine* is damaged in a collision with the Lowestoft side trawler *Roy Stevens* while fishing 300 miles east of Aberdeen. The seiner's bow was caved in and pumps were rushed out by helicopter. There was little damage to the *Roy Stevens*.

Skipper Bill Bridge breaks the Boston Group's earnings record for Fleetwood when he lands 1,649 kits to make £19,200. He took *Boston Blenheim* to Iceland for 21 a day trip and was harassed by the gunboat *Aegir*.

A message of thanks is sent to Iceland from Fleetwood for help given to the trawler *SSAFA* when she was badly damaged in mountainous seas. The Icelandic gunboat *Aegir* offered help. Skipper John Dunne of *SSAFA* said, "When it comes to seamen in danger the Icelanders forgot all that cod war nonsense".

For the third time this year the earnings record for the 90ft. class trawlers has been broken – this time by *Boston Scimitar* under Skipper G. DeBlock. Her 2,890st. catch sold for £2,233.

The 373 ton Hull trawler *Darthema* runs aground near Hekkinggen lighthouse 30 miles east of Tromso, north Norway. She radios for immediate assistance but later refloats without damage.

The fleetwood trawler *Boston Typhoon* returns from a 17 day trip to the Norwegian coast hake grounds with 6,680st. of fish, including 3,700st. of hake. Skipper Jack Chard grosses £4,200.

The new Hull distant water trawler *Princess Elizabeth* fails to cover the cost of her maiden voyage. She sailed from her home port on October 22 and fished mainly on around the Skolton Bank in the White Sea. The vessel lands 1,760 kits, consisting of of 1,000 of cod, 700 of haddock and 60 mixed. The catch realised £5,200 but a loss of £270 was incurred.

It is highly unlikely that the World Court catch limit off Iceland will be reached this year which means that British trawlers should not now have to withdraw from the area later this year to comply with the court.

The court requested Britain to reduce her total catch off Iceland to 170,000 tons a year but this is not now expected to be reached.

Meanwhile there was another collision between a navy

frigate and an Icelandic gunboat. The Hull trawler *Kingston Jade* was being protected by the frigate *Arethusa* when in collision with Iceland's *Odinn*.

Below is a list of the Boston Empire, the companies which over the years came under their control:

Boston Deep Sea Fisheries. Previously, Boston Deep Sea Fishing & Ice Co. Ltd. (The parent company).
St. Andrew's Steam Fishing Co.
Aberdeen Motor Trawlers.
Aberdeen Near Water Trawlers Ltd.
Acadia Fisheries Ltd., Halifax and St. Johns, Canada.
Adam Steam Fishing Co. Ltd.
Barbara Steam Fishing Co. Ltd.
Bay Fisheries Ltd.
Bloctube Controls Ltd.
Brixham Trawlers Ltd.
Carry on Fishing Co. Ltd.
Dominion Fishing Co. Ltd.
Don Fishing Co. Ltd.
Eager Fishing Co. Ltd.
Eddystone Fishing Co. Ltd.
Fleetwood Near Water Trawlers Ltd.
Gilbert & Co. Ltd.
Grimsby Near Water Trawlers.
Iago Steam Trawlers Co. Ltd.
W. H. Kerr (Ship Chandlers).
Looker Fishing Co. Ltd.
Lowestoft Fish Selling Co. Ltd.
Mastyn & Willy Ltd.
Near Water Trawlers Ltd.
Neptune Steam Fishing Co. Ltd.
North Cape S.F.
North Shore Fishing Co. Ltd.
Onward Fishing Co. Ltd.
Parbell-Smith Ltd.
Pecheries De La Morinie, Boulogne.
Pegasus Trawling Co. Ltd.
Pentode Ltd.
Robins Trawlers Ltd.
F.&T. Ross Ltd.
St. Christopher Steam Fishing Co. Ltd.
Star Drift Fishing Co. Ltd.
Universal Motor Trawlers Ltd.

Universal Trawlers Ltd.
Weelsby Trawlers Ltd.
Wellbottom (Trawlers) Ltd.
Wiltapas Ltd.

Marine Steam Fishing Co. Ltd.
Eton Fishing Co. Ltd.
Alliance Steam Fishing Co. Ltd.
J.C. Llewellin (Milford Haven) Ltd.
Great Western Fishing Co. Ltd.
Grimsby Trawlers Ltd.
Grimsby Fish Meal Company.
Industrial & Maritime Riggers Ltd.
Tyne Wire Rope Co. Ltd.
United Towing Co. Ltd.
North British Finance Co. Ltd.
Hull Gate Shipping Co. Ltd.

And so a great Company came to the end of its days. Sir Basil Parkes retired in 1978 when he sold all his shares in the company. He moved to the Isle of Man where he enjoyed his retirement in peaceful surroundings. His son Fred formed a company called Fred Parkes Holdings Ltd., which he ran successfully until he too followed his father into retirement in 1979, and moved to the Isle of Man. Neil also disposed of his shares but bought land in East Yorkshire from the company, where he still resides, controlling large agricultural interests.